BIG BOOK OF MAZES

Andrews McMeel Publishing

Kansas City • Sydney • London

Andrews McMeel Publishing, LLC
an Andrews McMeel Universal company
1130 Walnut Street, Kansas City, Missouri 64106

www.andrewsmcmeel.com

All puzzles supplied under license from Puzzler Media Ltd.
www.puzzler.com

15 16 17 18 PAH 10 9 8 7 6 5 4 3 2

ISBN: 978-1-4494-6485-1

Made by:
The P. A. Hutchison Company
Address and location of production:
400 Penn Avenue, Mayfield, PA 18433 USA
2nd printing – 2/27/15

1
Autograph Hunter

Find your way from start to finish without crossing any solid lines.

2

Circus Trail

Can you find the correct arrow trail to help this man get to the baby elephant that is lost?

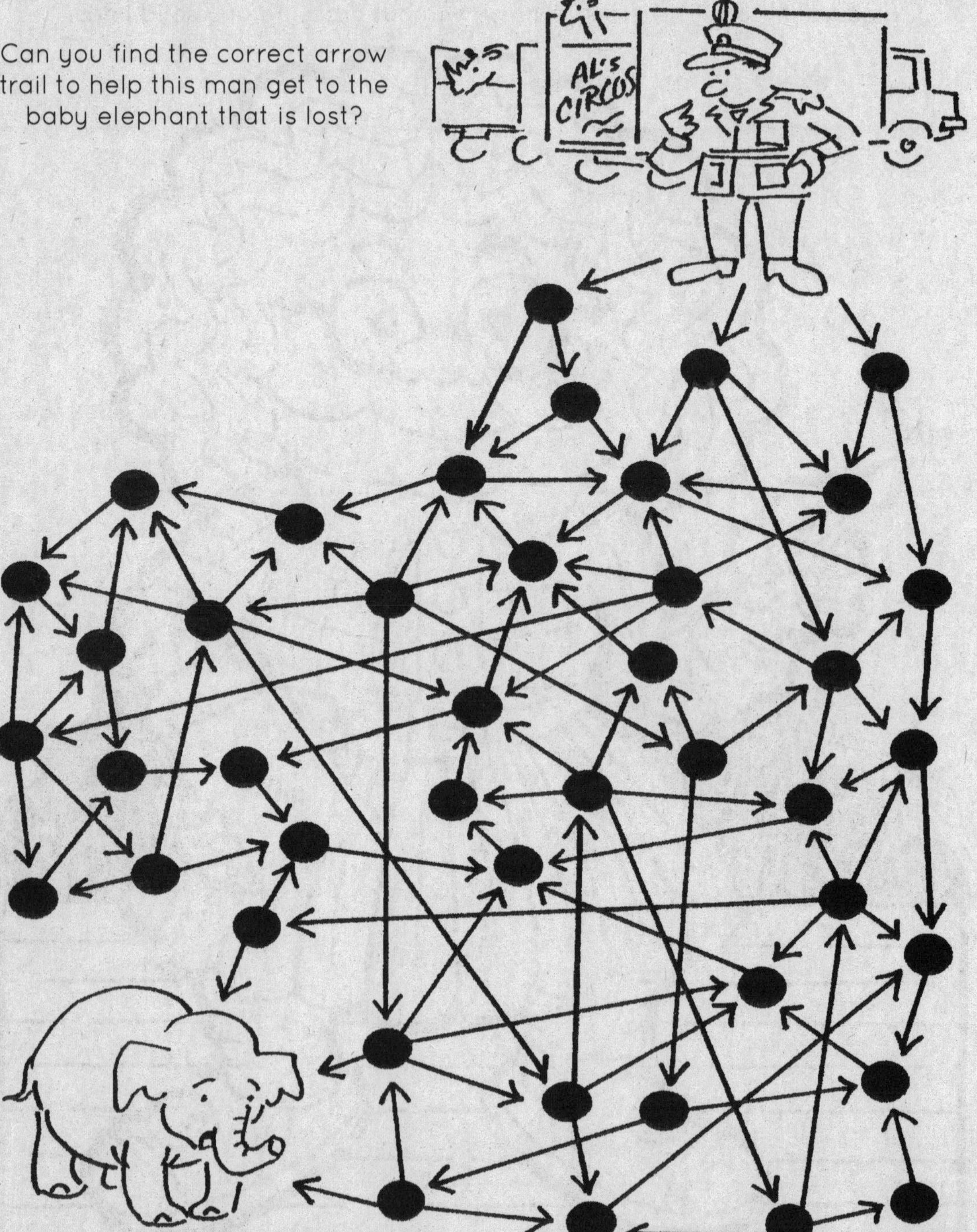

3
Mobile Maze

See if you can find your way through this maze from the rabbit to the other cell phone.

4

Alien Puzzle

Can you follow a line from start to finish in one continuous movement?

5

Hop to It

Help this girl get through the maze to rescue her pet frog.

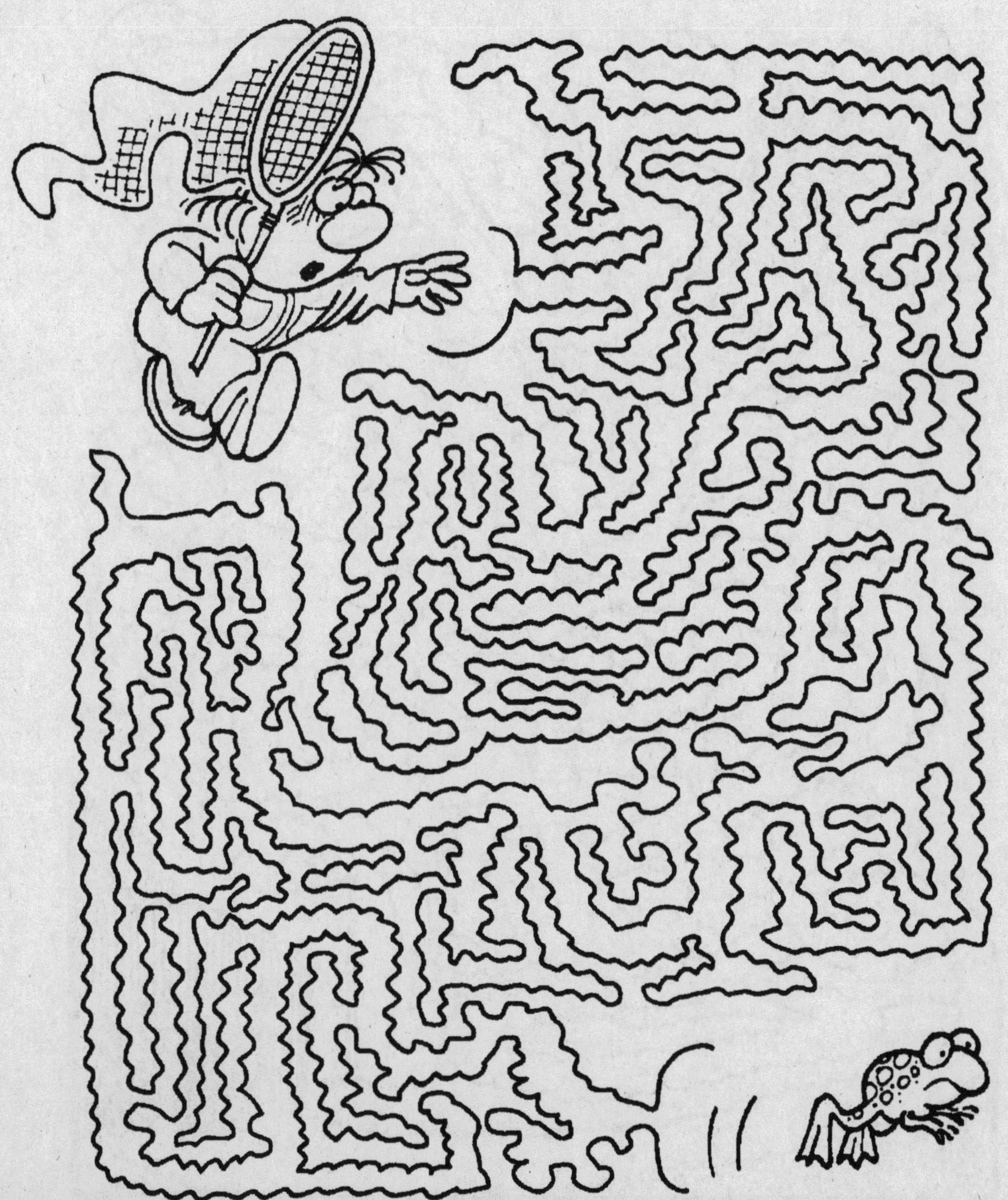

6

Flight Path

Help this cat find his way back to the hangar.

7

Space Race

Can you find the correct arrow trail to help these alien tourists get to Earth and avoid the meteor shower?

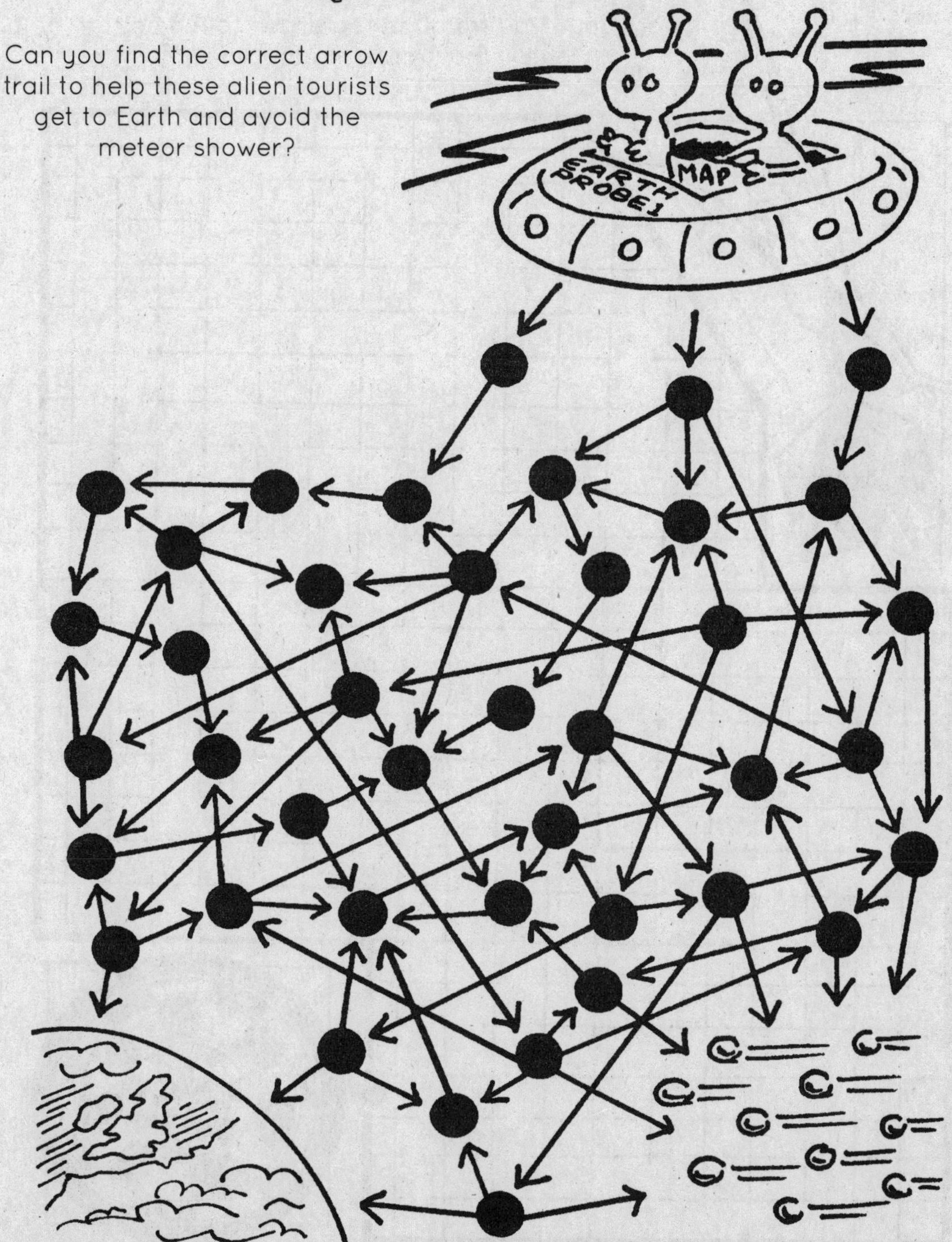

8

Board Game

Work your way from the top arrow to the bottom one without crossing any lines.

9

Rabbit Route

Can you follow a line from start to finish in one continuous movement?

10

Something Fishy

Only one of these fish makes it through the maze to the bottom. Can you work out which one it is?

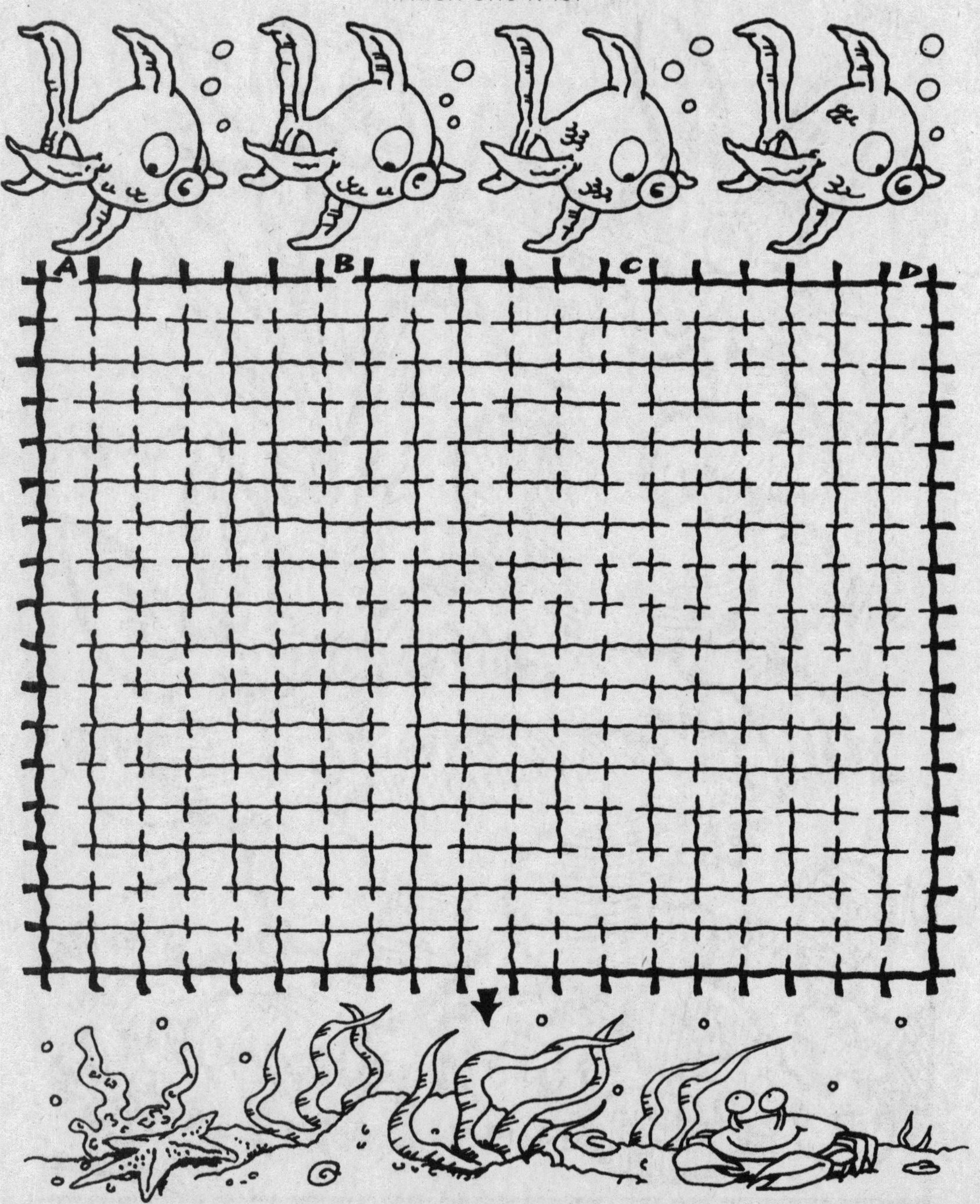

11

Wiz Bizz

See if you can lead the wizard through this maze from his feet to the dragon.

12

Science Test

Find a trail from the tap at the top to the beaker at the bottom.

13

Monkey Puzzle

Can you find the correct arrow trail to help this monkey get to the bananas and avoid the hunters?

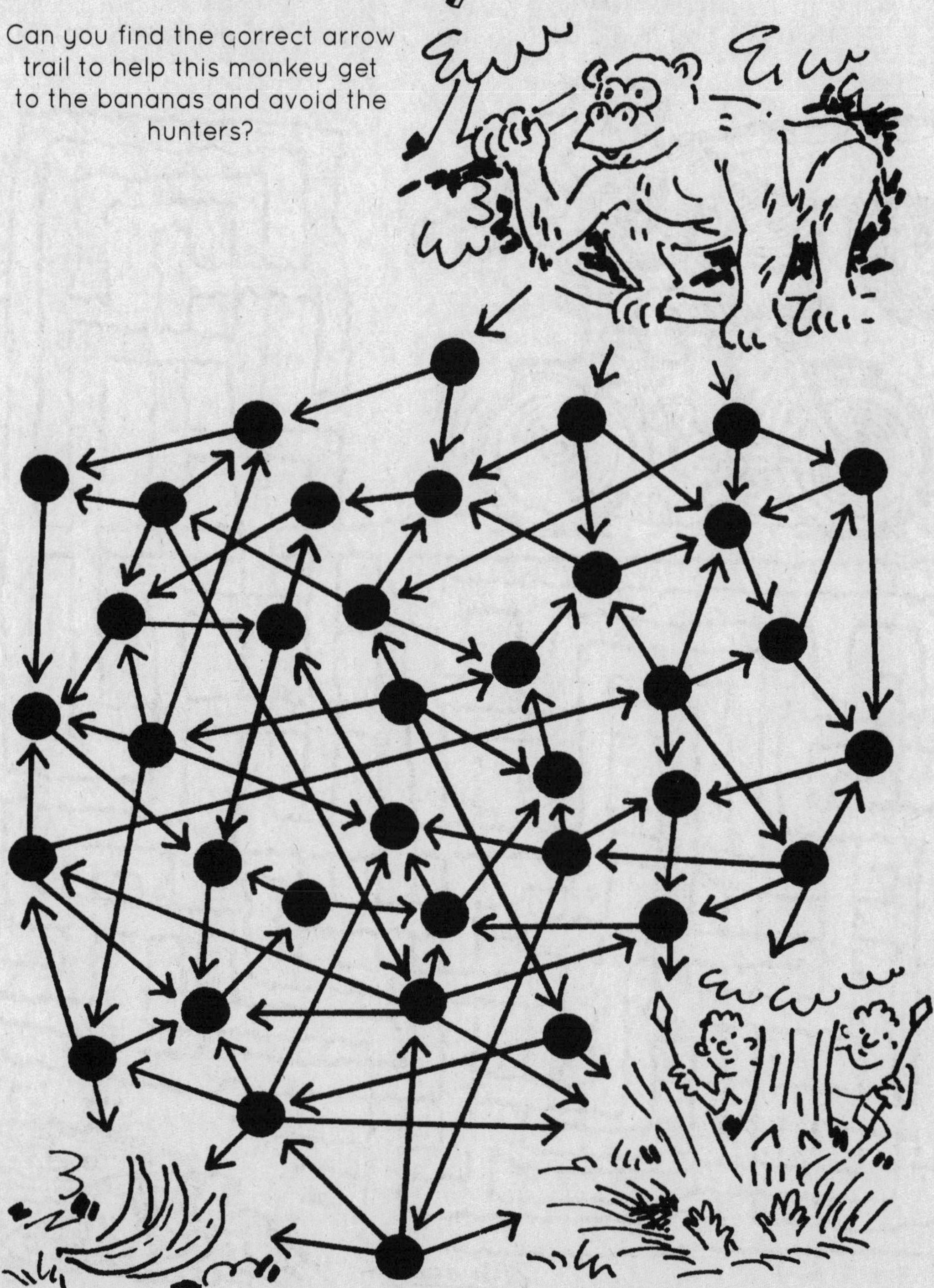

14
Cycle Path

Help this boy find a path to the river so he can go fishing.

15

Tool Box Trouble

See if you can get from the wrench to the nut.

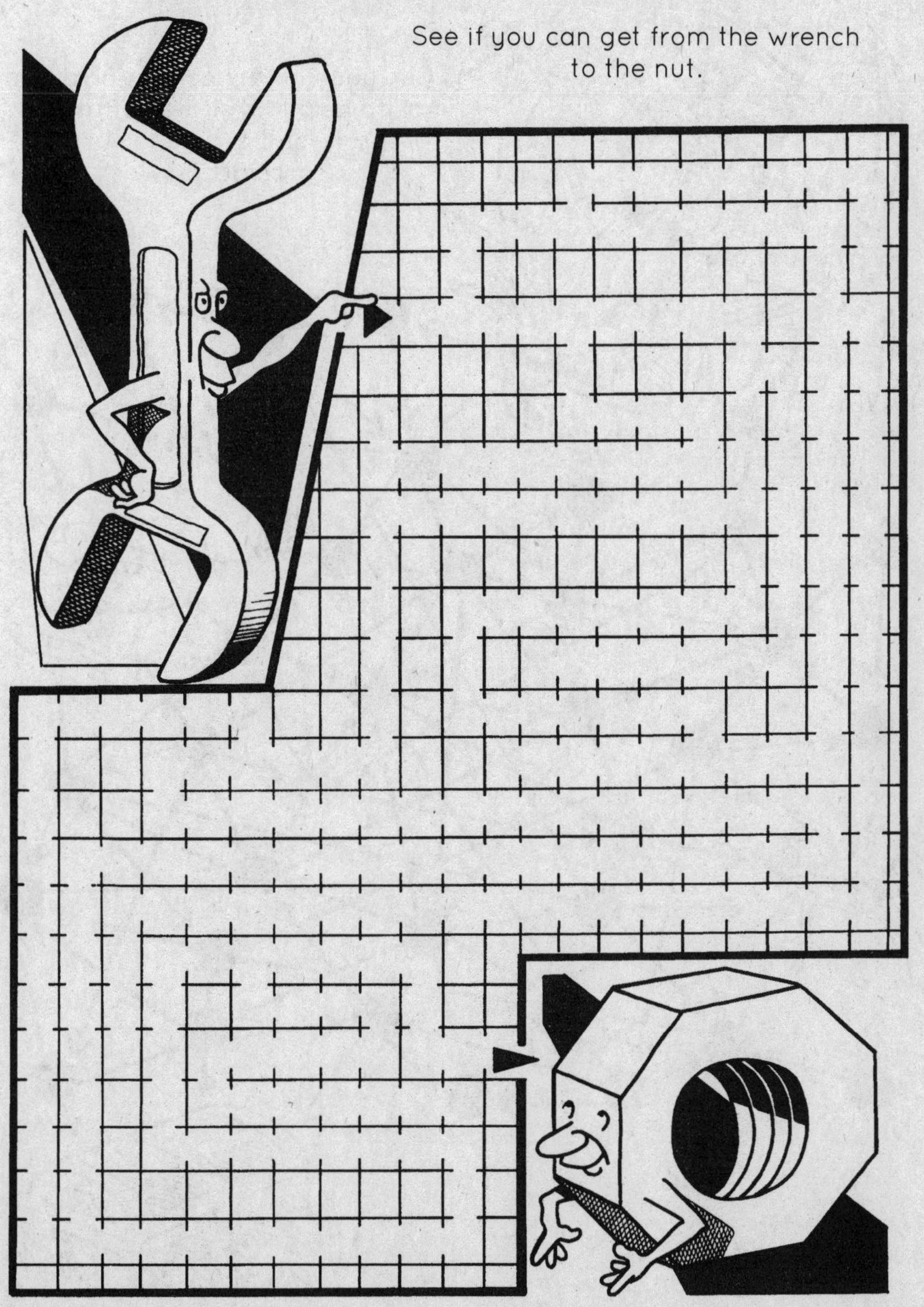

16

Treasure Hunt

Can you find the correct arrow trail to help this pirate get to his treasure and avoid the nasty spider?

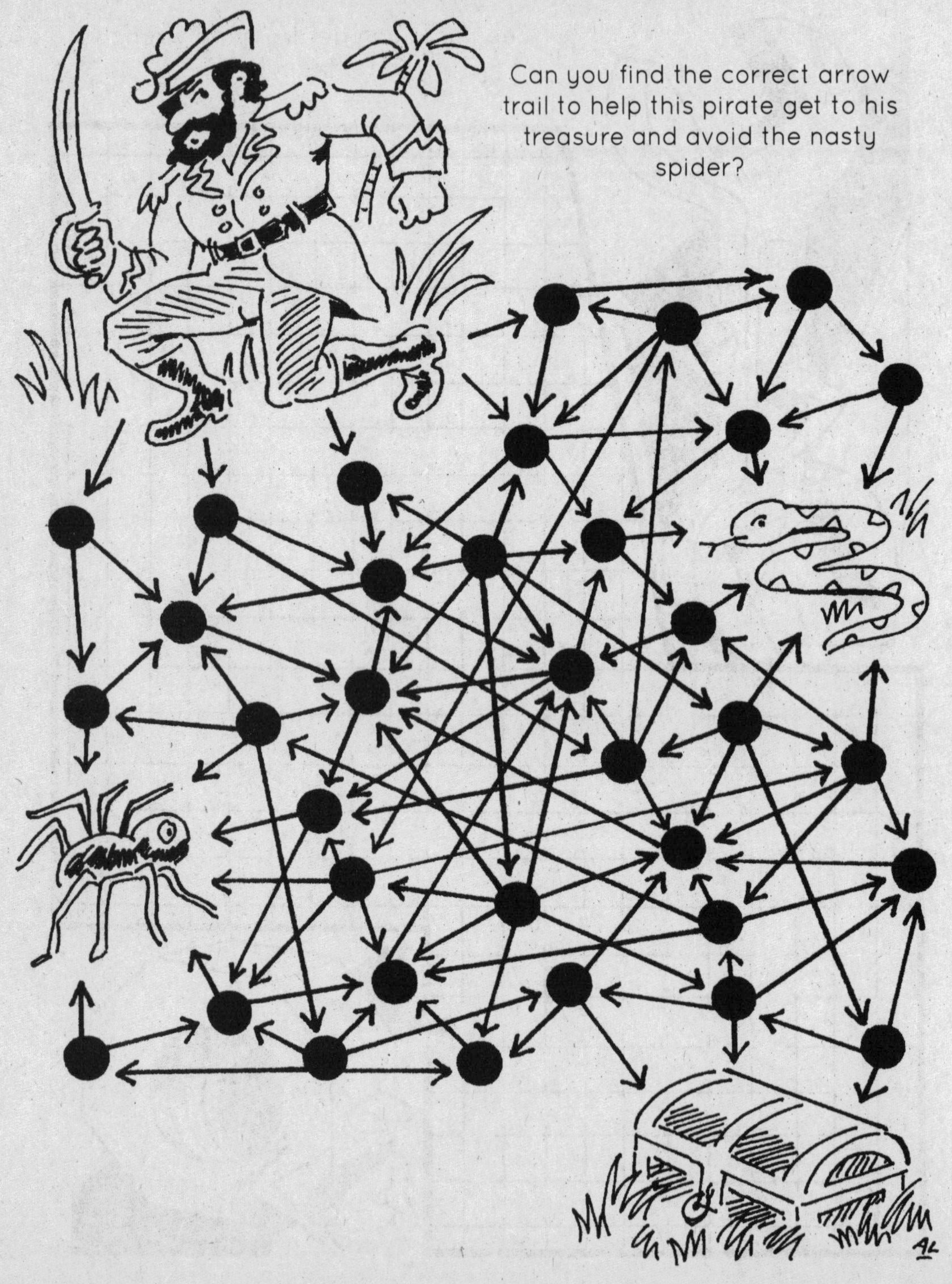

17
Blowing Bubbles

Find a path through the bubbles from the pipe to the bubble mix.

18
Jigsaw Puzzle

Try to get to the missing part of the jigsaw.

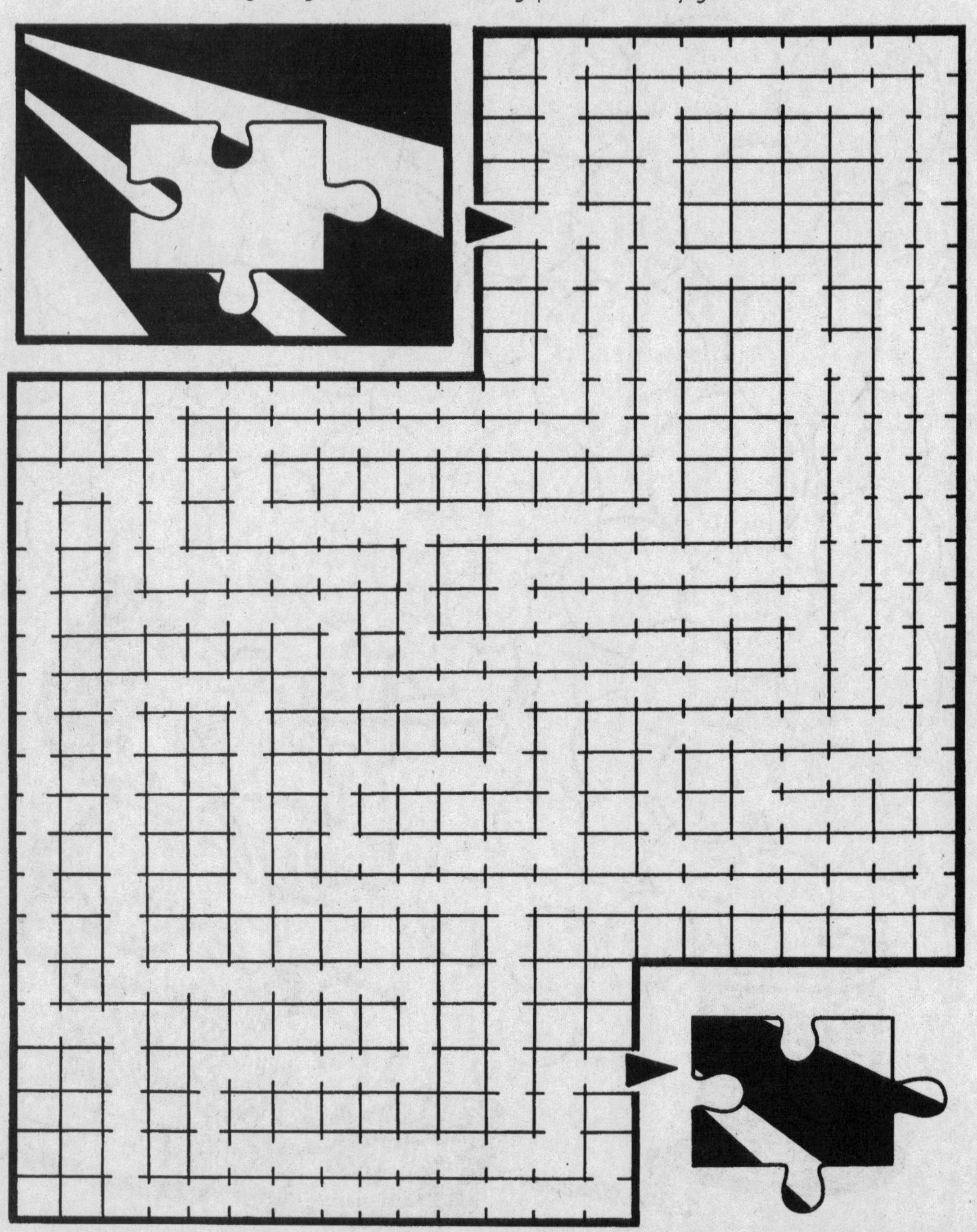

19

Neptune Trail

Find your way from start to finish without crossing any solid lines.

20
Rocket to Me

Can you find the correct arrow trail to help this astronaut get back to his spaceship and avoid the aliens?

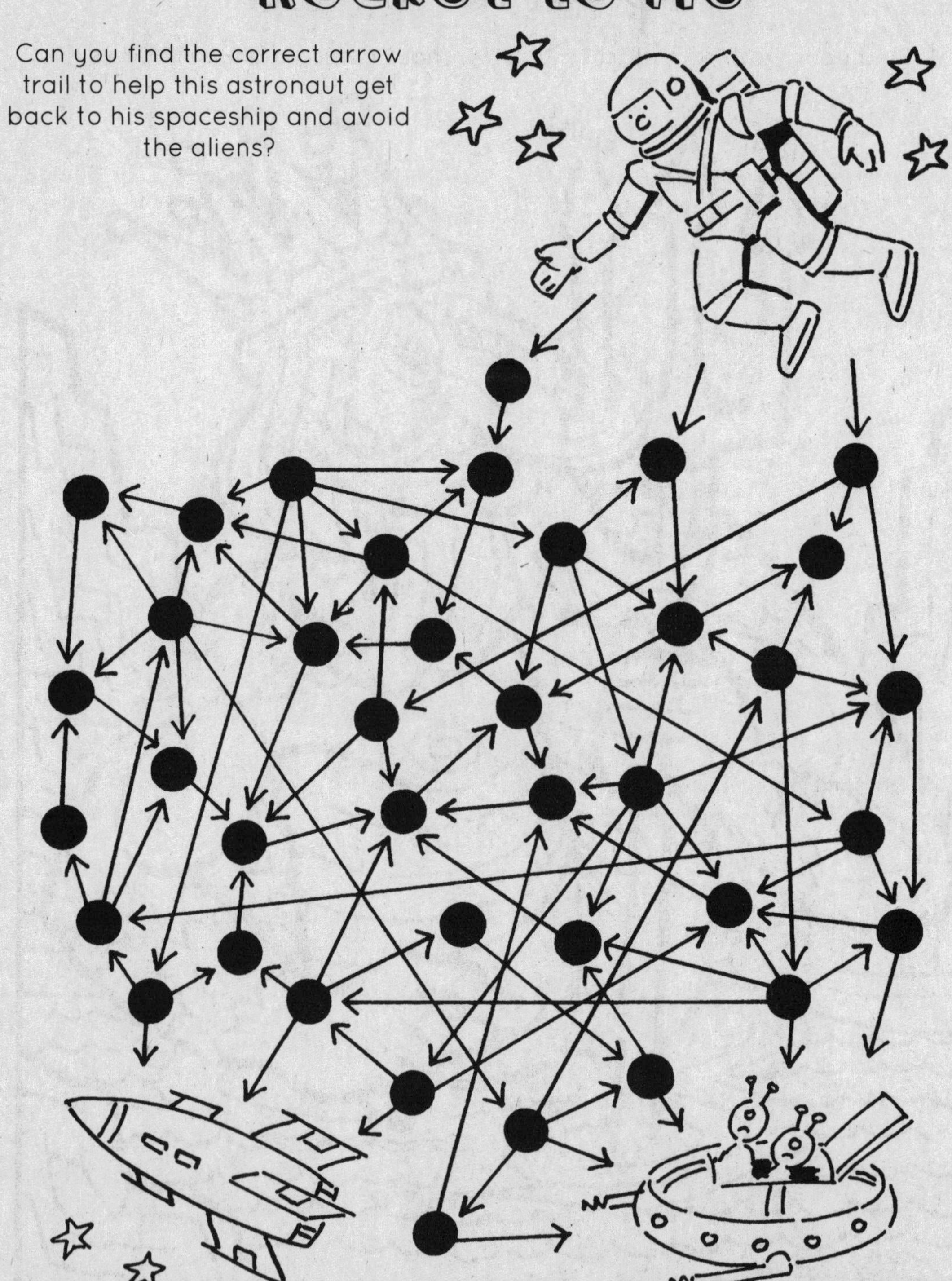

21

Mask Maze

Work your way through this scary mask without going over any solid lines.

22
Wagon Train

Can you find the correct arrow trail to help this stagecoach get back to town and avoid the outlaws?

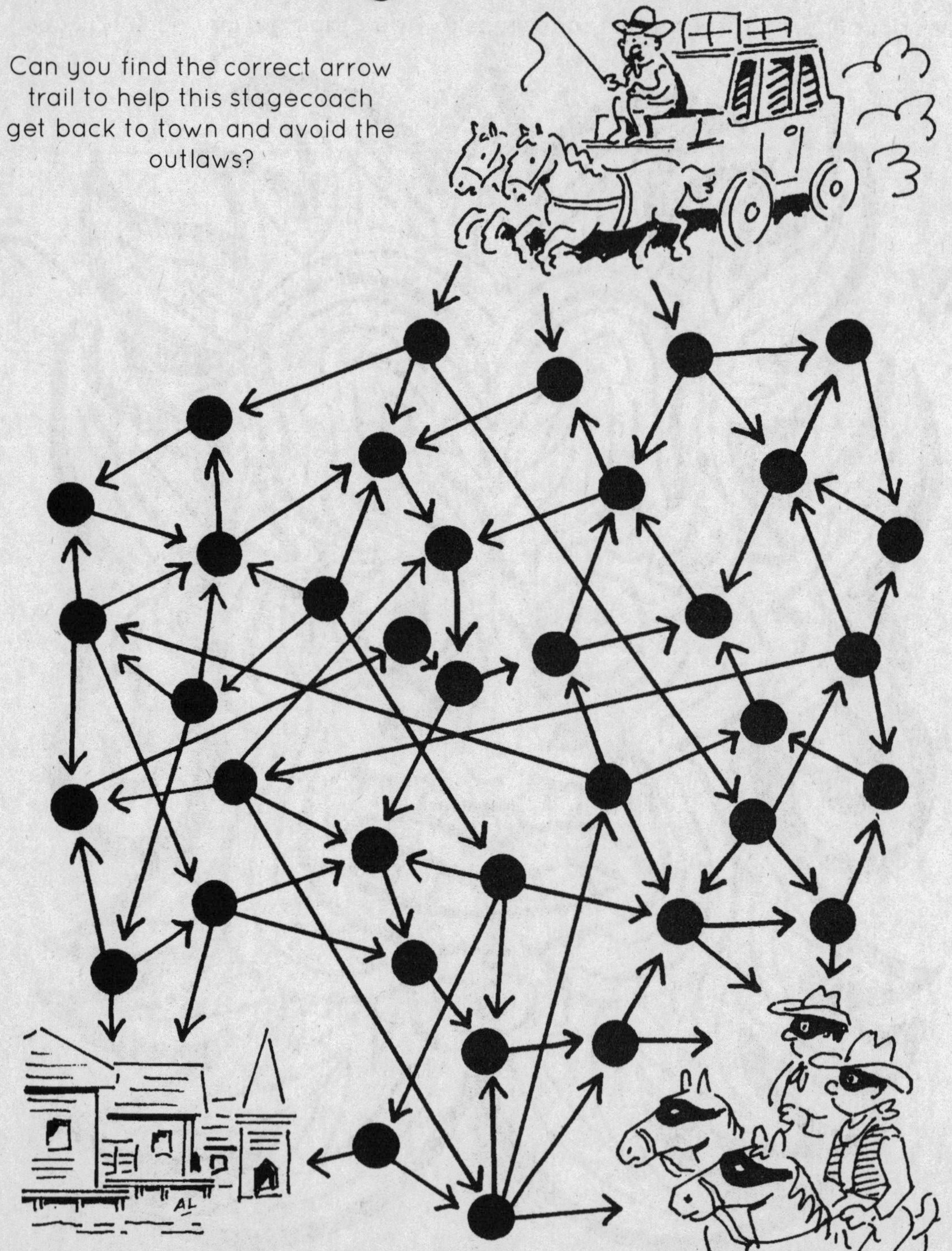

23
Car Wash

Can you find a path through this maze so the man goes to the car wash and back home again?

24

Burglar Bill

Burglar Bill wants to get to his loot, can you find a way through the maze?

25

Dragon Lines

Find your way from in to out without crossing any solid lines.

26
Rescue Package

Can you find the correct arrow trail to get the package to the man on the desert island and avoid the hungry shark?

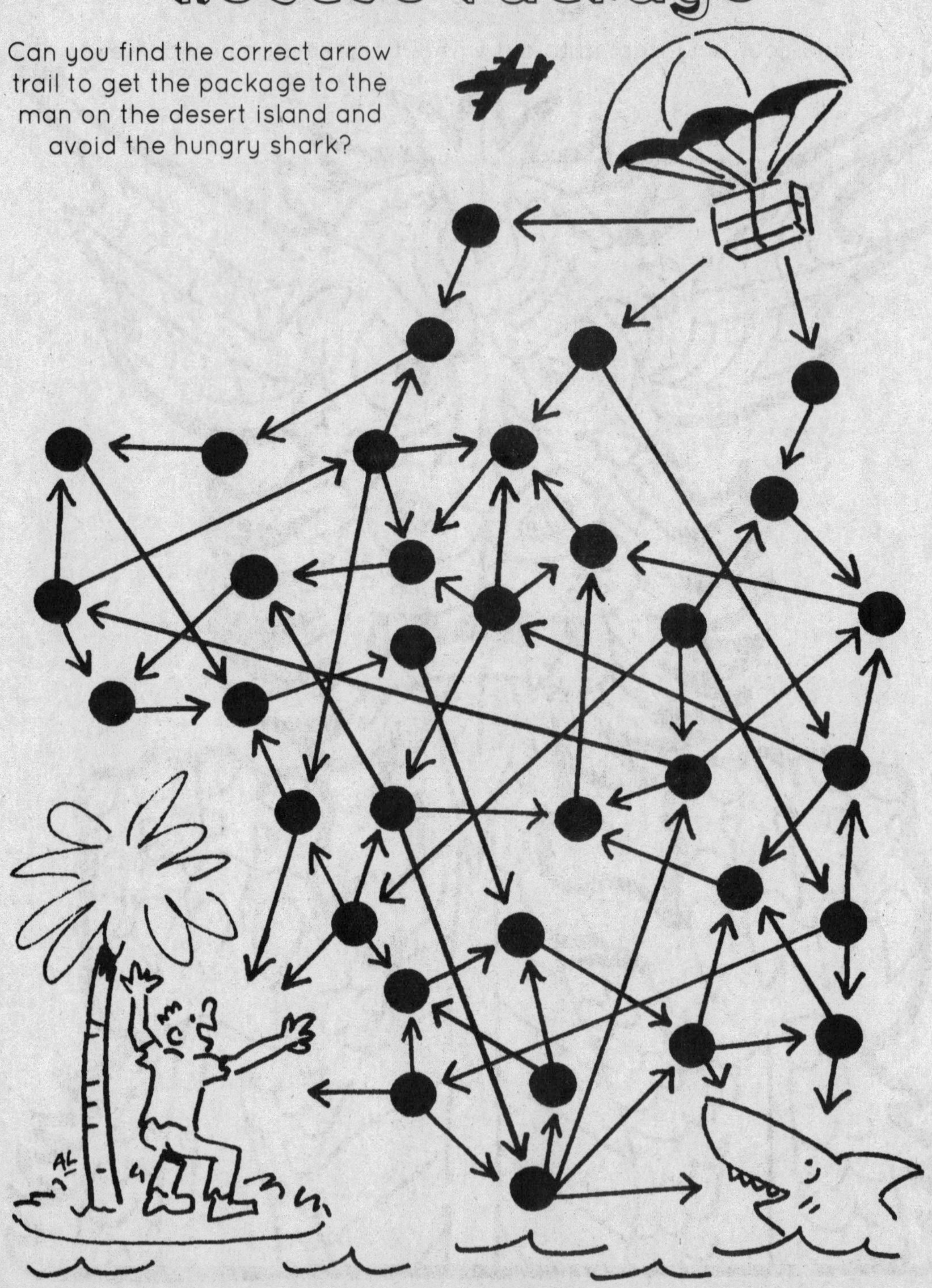

Jack and the Beanstalk

Help Jack climb up the beanstalk to the castle.

FINISH.

CLIFF ROWN

28
Panda Puzzle

Help this panda get through this maze to get to his bamboo.

29
Diamond Hunters

Which trail should these explorers take to get to the diamond mine?

30

Big Bang

Can you find the correct arrow trail to get this man to the water tank and avoid the tree?

31
Tennis Trail

Can you follow a line from start to finish in one continuous movement?

32
Car Trouble

See if you can work out how to get this couple to the beach.

33
Hair Raising

Only one of the trails leading from A to D leads to the exit. Can you work out which one it is?

34
Turtle Trail

Find your way from start to finish without crossing any solid lines.

35

Kite Trouble

Can you find a path through this maze to get to the box kite?

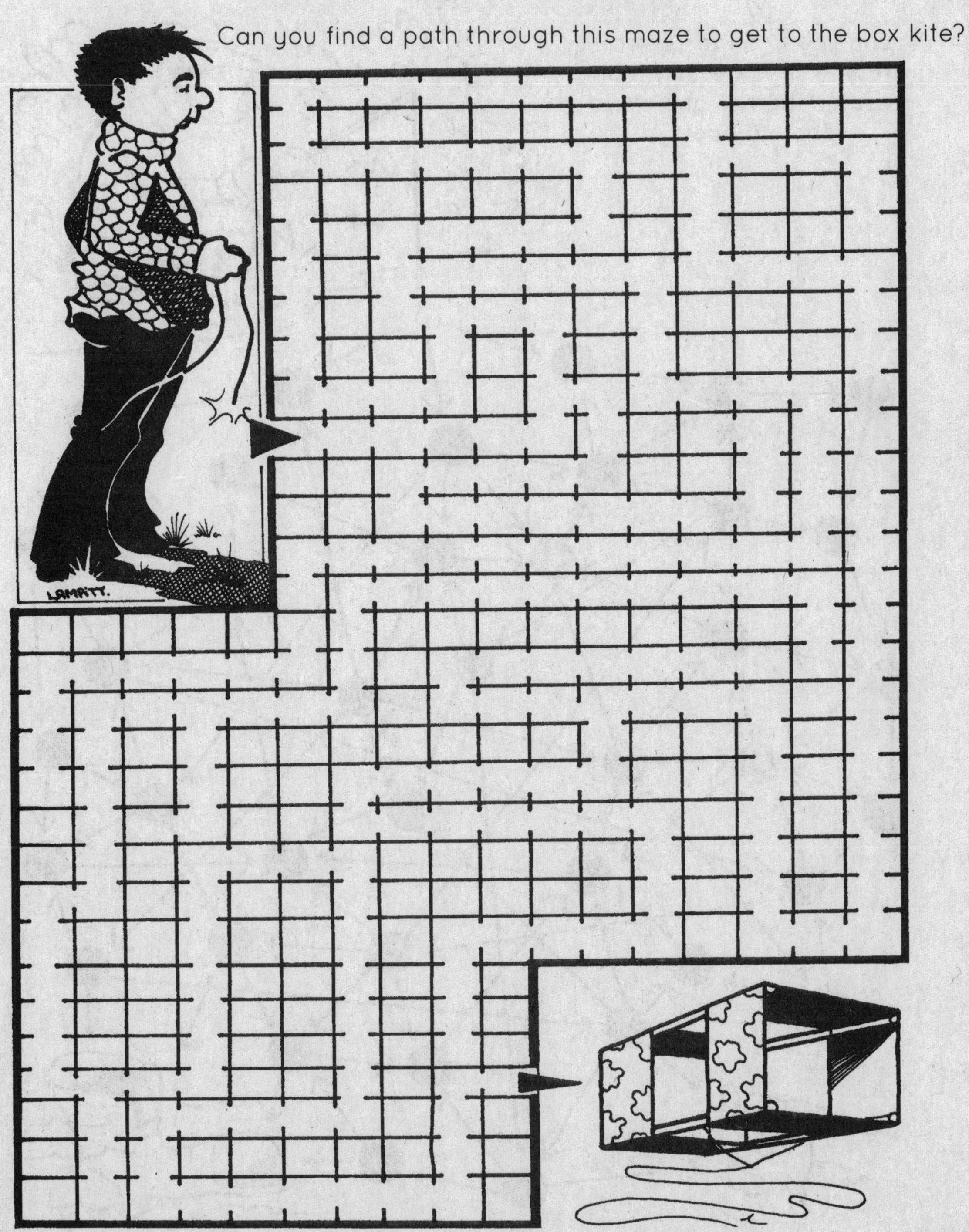

36

Fishing Line

Can you find the correct arrow trail to get this man to catch the fish and avoid the old boot?

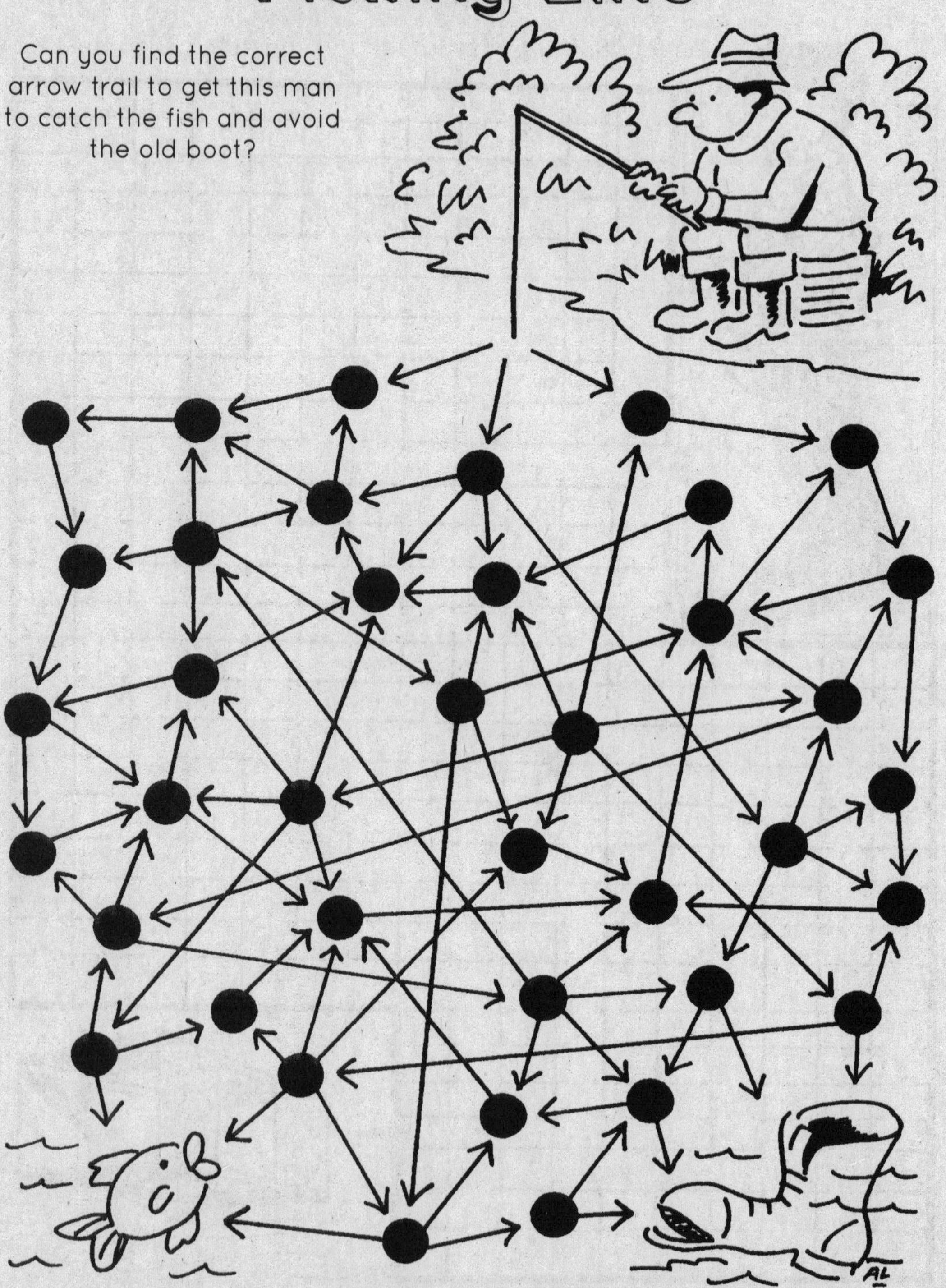

37

Here Kitty Kitty

Help this kitten find its way through the maze to its mother.

38

Leaf Me Alone

Find a way to get the leaf through the maze to the wheelbarrow.

LAMPITT

39

Bicycle Lane

This boy wants to get home avoiding the hazards. Can you help him out?

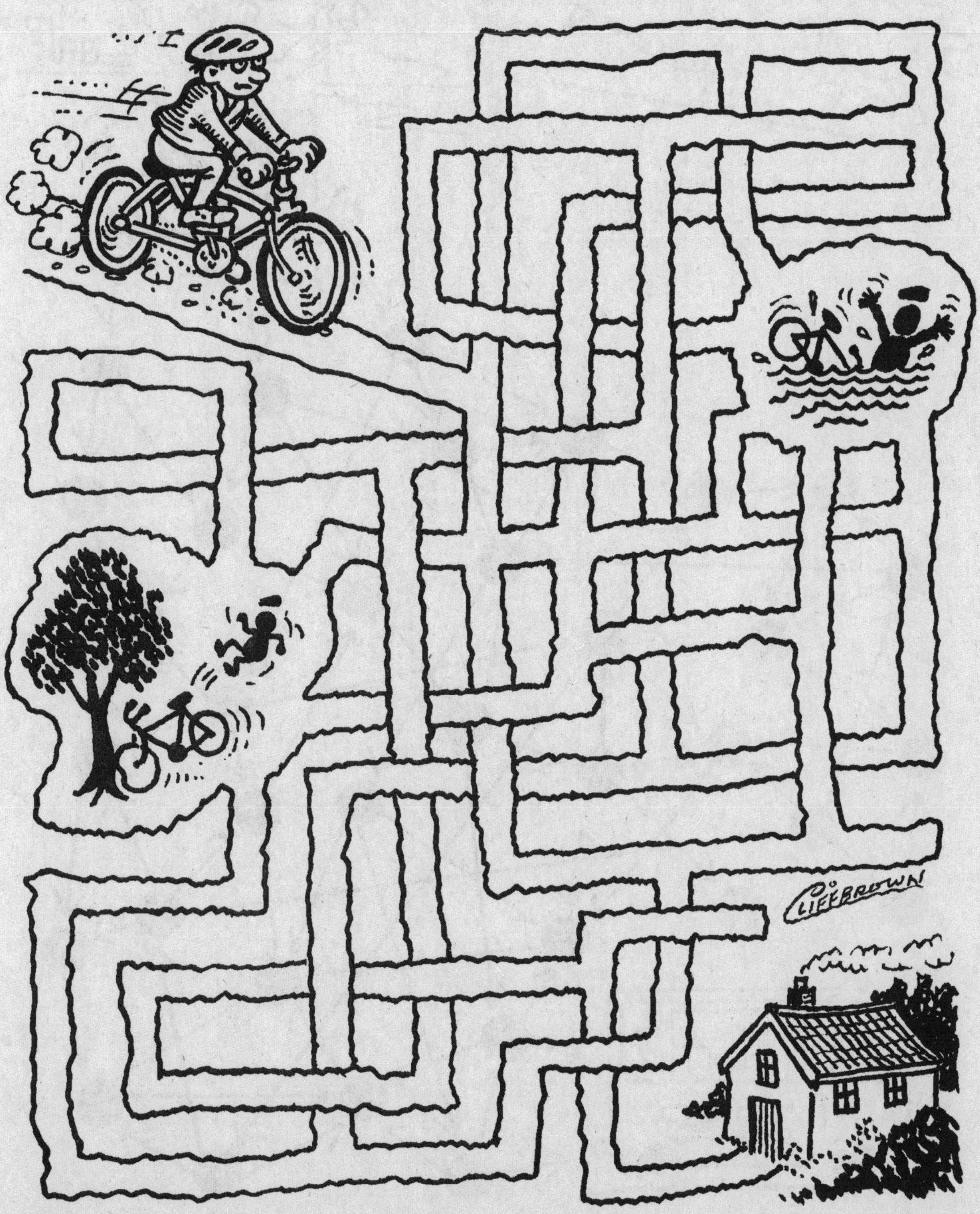

40

I Scream

Can you find the correct arrow trail to get this boy to the ice cream van?

41
Spider Web

Help this spider get through the web to get to the fly.

42

Fruit Basket

These bananas need to get back to the fruit basket.
Can you help them out?

43

Rabbit Run

Help this rabbit get back home avoiding the hungry wolf.

44
Arrow Puzzle

Can you find the correct arrow trail to get the arrow to the target and avoid the greenhouse?

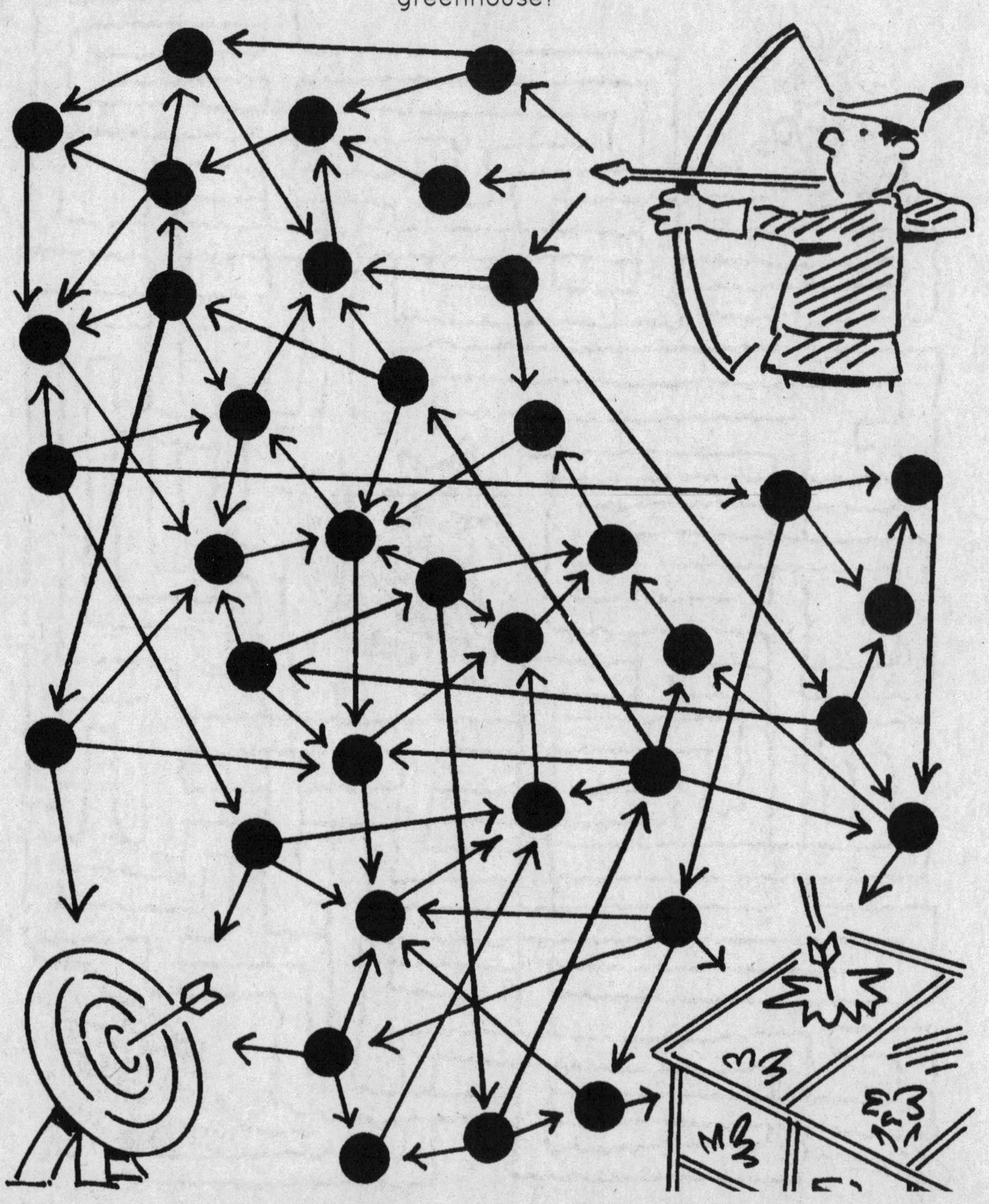

45
Clowning Around

Find your way from start to finish without crossing any solid lines.

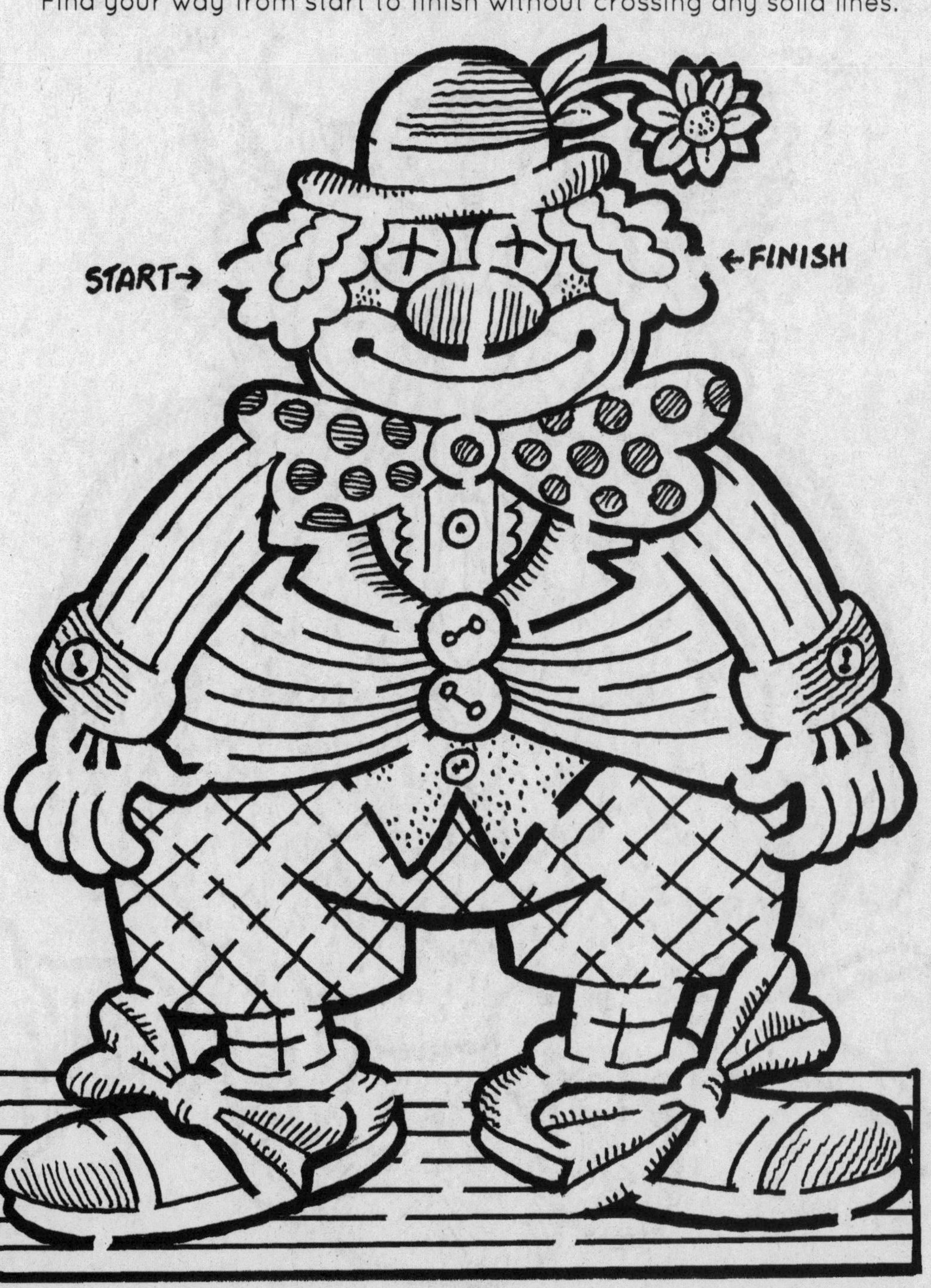

46

Give a Hoot

Can you follow a line from start to finish in one continuous movement?

47

Pirate Path

Can you find the correct arrow trail to get the pirates to the treasure and avoid the angry natives?

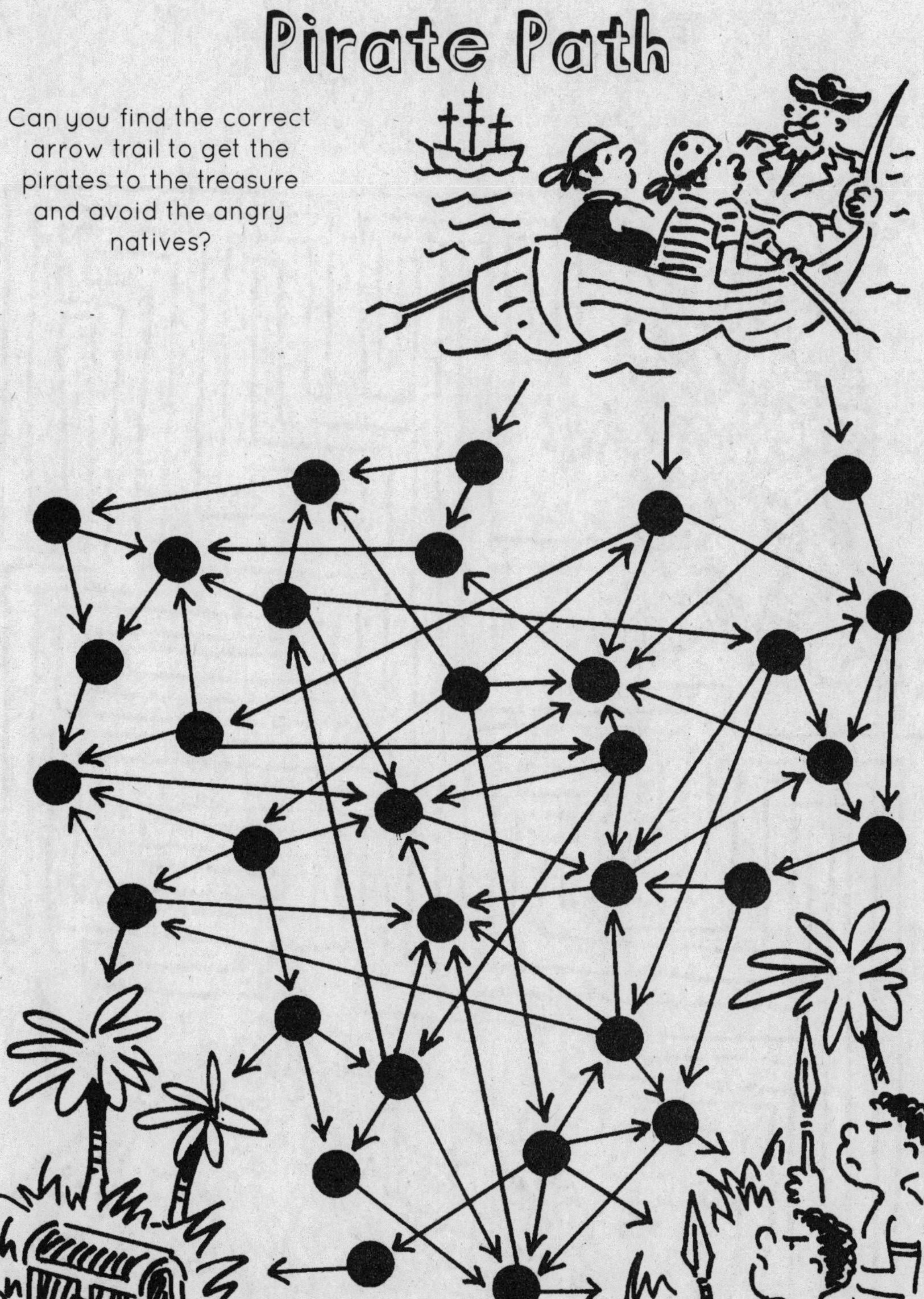

48

Fright Knight

This silly knight wants to fight the dragon. Can you help him find a path through the maze?

49

Bird Brain

Help this bird get to the feeder by finding a way through the maze.

50

Pirate Pete

Pirate Pete has lost his treasure map. Can you help him find his way to the treasure chest?

51

Bee Line

Can you follow a line from the bee's leg to the cherry on the slice of cake in one continuous movement?

52
Ship Shape

Can you find the correct arrow trail to help this ship get to the island and avoid the jagged rocks?

53
Musical Maze

Can you follow a line from one arrow to the other in one continuous movement?

54

Flower Power

Find a way to get the bee through the maze to the flower.

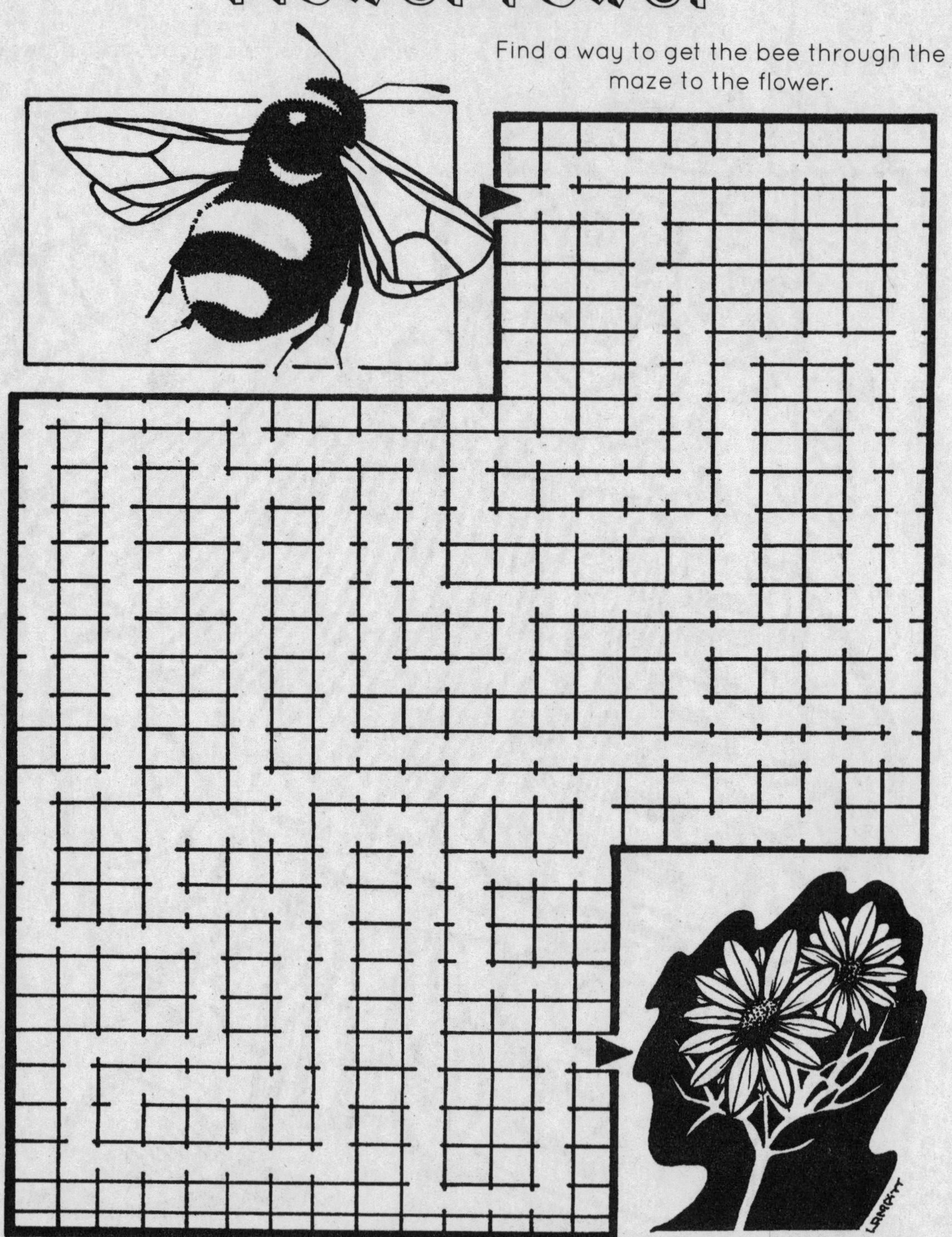

55

Dino Pet

Can you find the correct arrow trail to help this caveman get to his pet dinosaur?

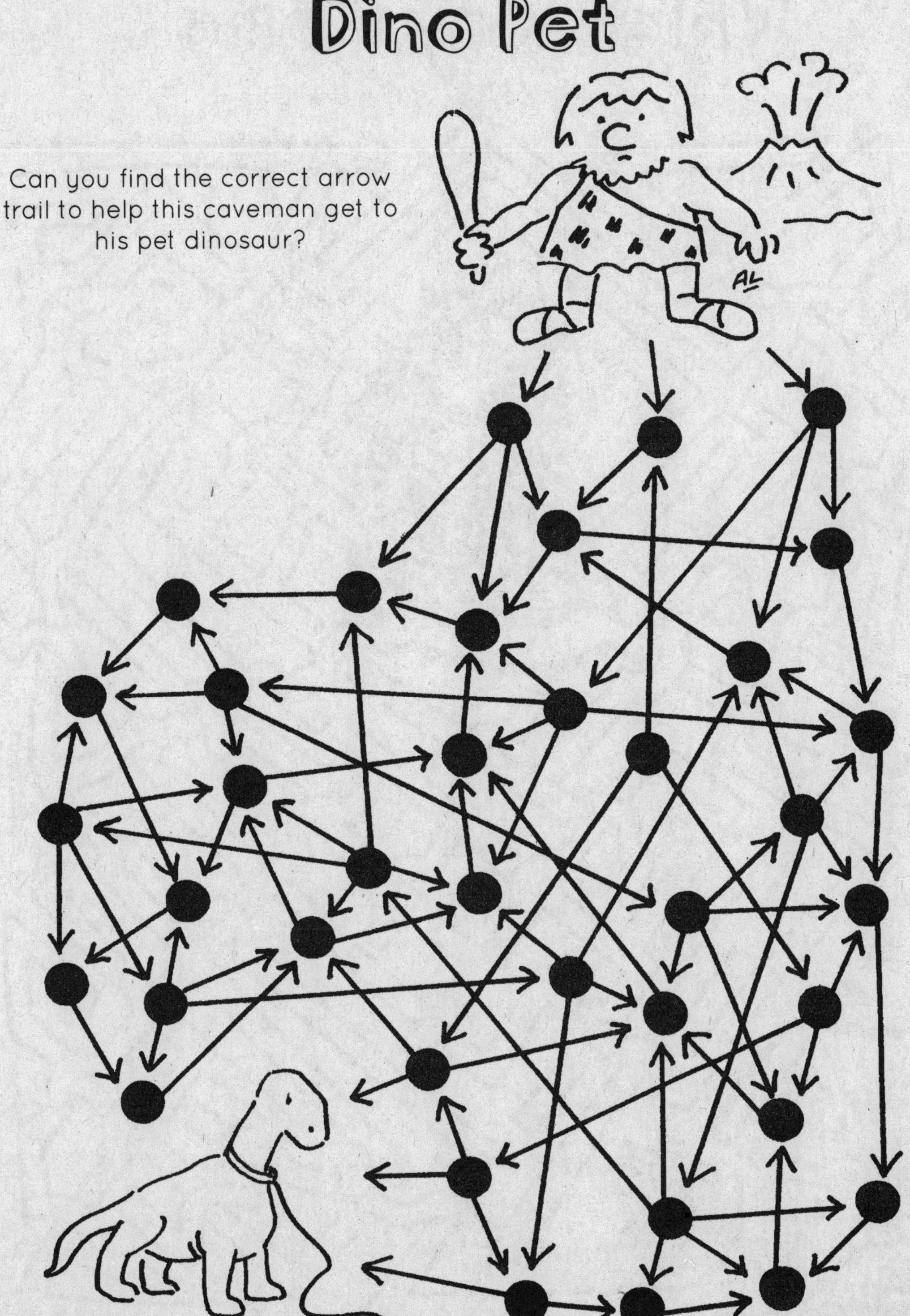

56

Which Way Home?

Try to help this lost boy find his way home.

57

Gone Fishing

Can you follow a line from start to the fish in one continuous movement?

58

Camel Trail

Find your way from start to finish without crossing any solid lines.

59
Bunny Builder

This rabbit needs one more brick to finish his wall. Can you help him through the maze to get to it?

60

Roman Around

Can you find the correct arrow trail to help this Roman soldier get back home?

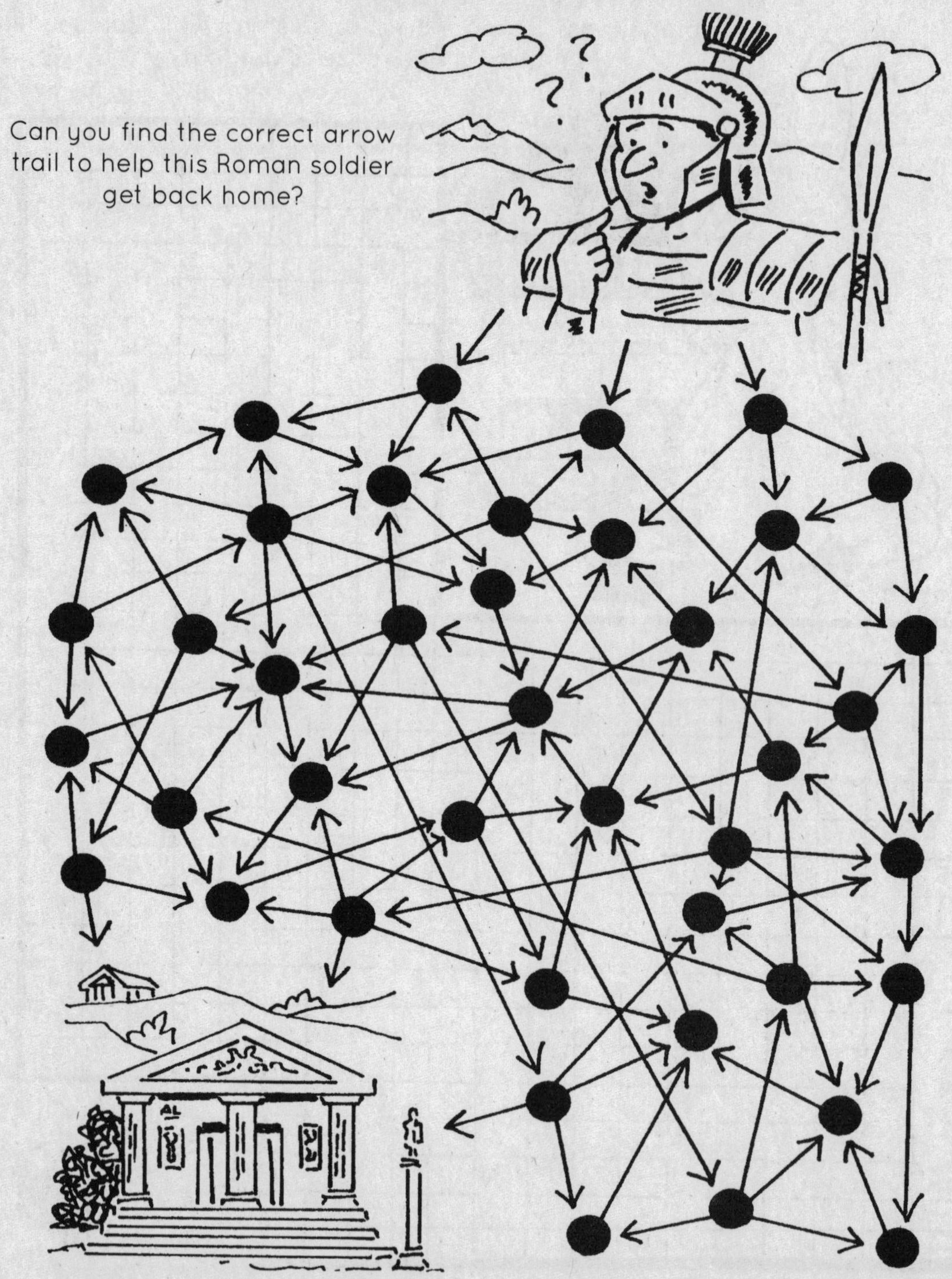

61

Parachute Path

Find the path to help this man parachute safely onto the ground.

62
Creature Feature

Can you follow a line from start to finish in one continuous movement?

63

Horsing Around

Find a path through the maze to get this horse to its saddle.

64

Mountain Path

Help these men find a way to the top of the mountain and back down again avoiding the angry mountain goat.

65
Hey Presto!

Can you find the correct arrow trail to help this wizard get to his pet lizard which he made disappear?

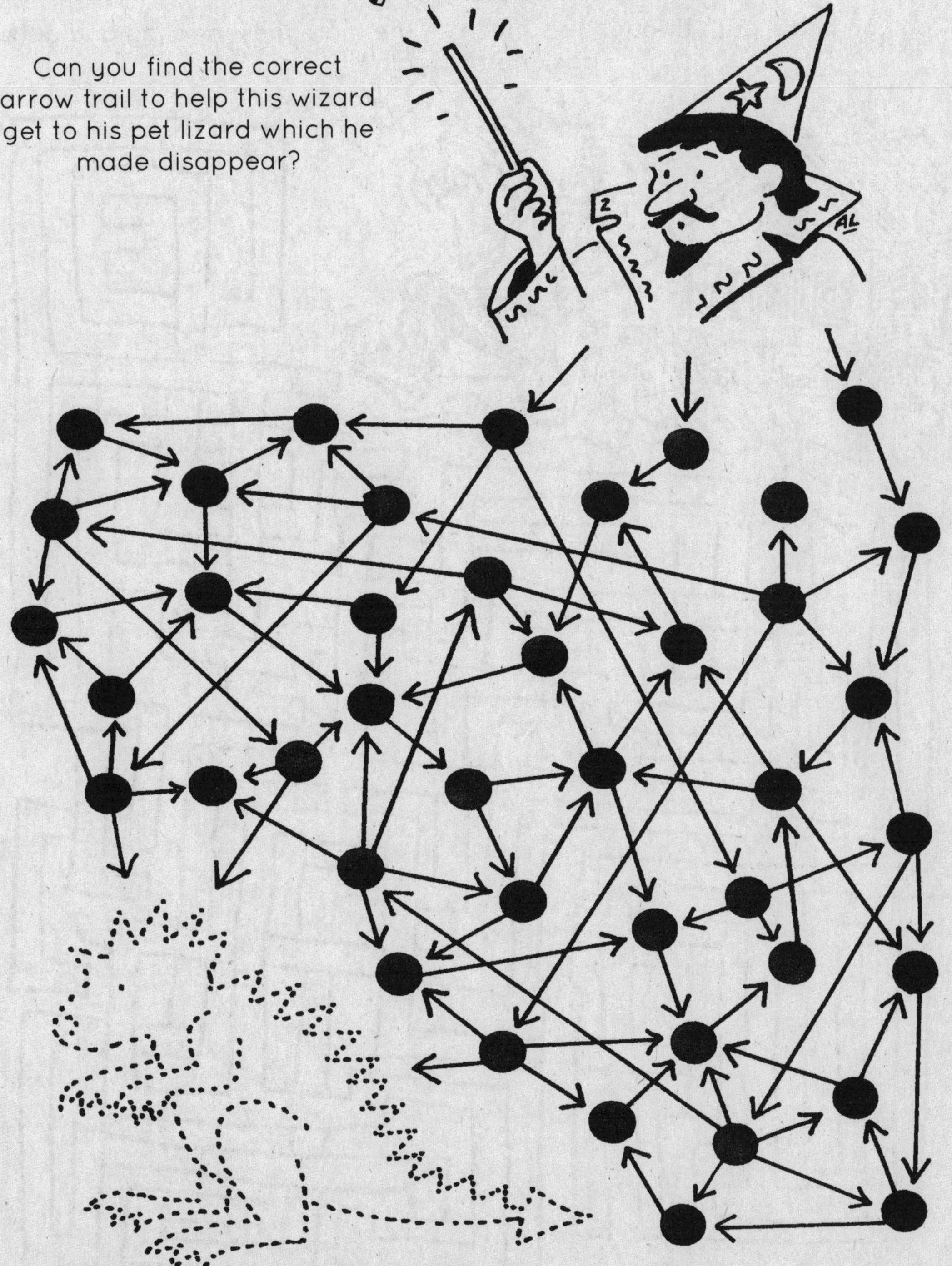

66
Running Track

Can you find a path through this maze so the man goes for a jog and gets back home again?

67
Fishing Line

Can you follow a line from start to the tasty worm in one continuous movement?

Flashlight Find

Work your way through the maze to get to the flashlight battery.

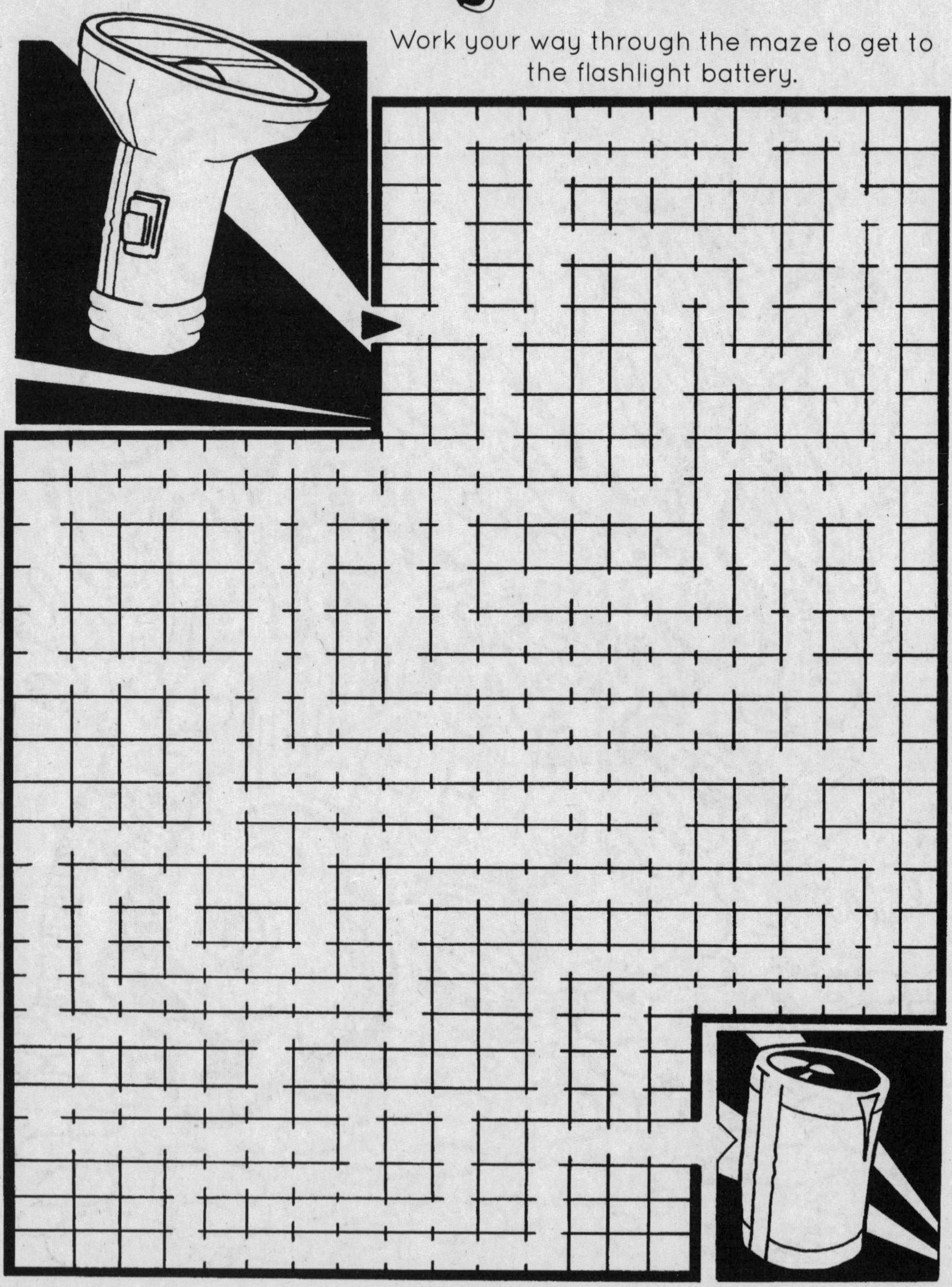

69

Hot Dog

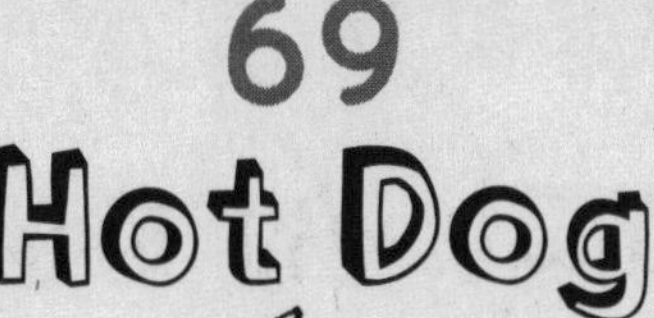

Can you find the correct arrow trail to help Bonzo get to his bone before the cat runs off with it?

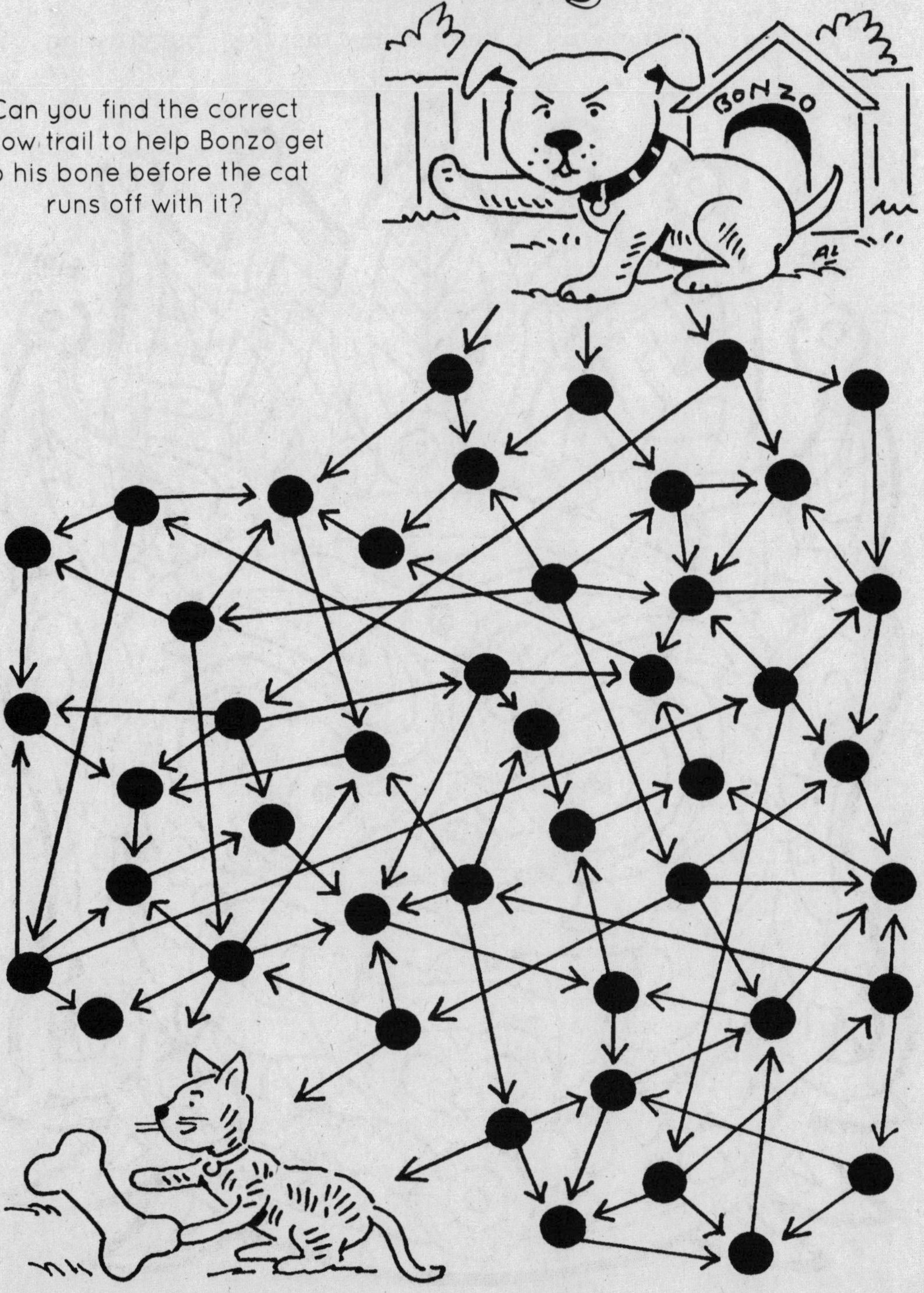

70
Mask Around

Find your way from start to finish on this mask without crossing any solid lines.

High Flyer

Help this boy get through the maze to his remote control plane.

72
Skating in a Line

Can you follow a line from start to finish in one continuous movement?

73

Witch Path?

Help Wanda the witch find her way through the maze to get to her broom.

74

Fan-tastic

Can you find the correct arrow trail to help these fans get to their favorite pop star?

75
Gordon the Ghost

Help Gordon the ghost find his way to his head.

76

Pooch Path

Help get this hungry pooch through the maze to his juicy bone.

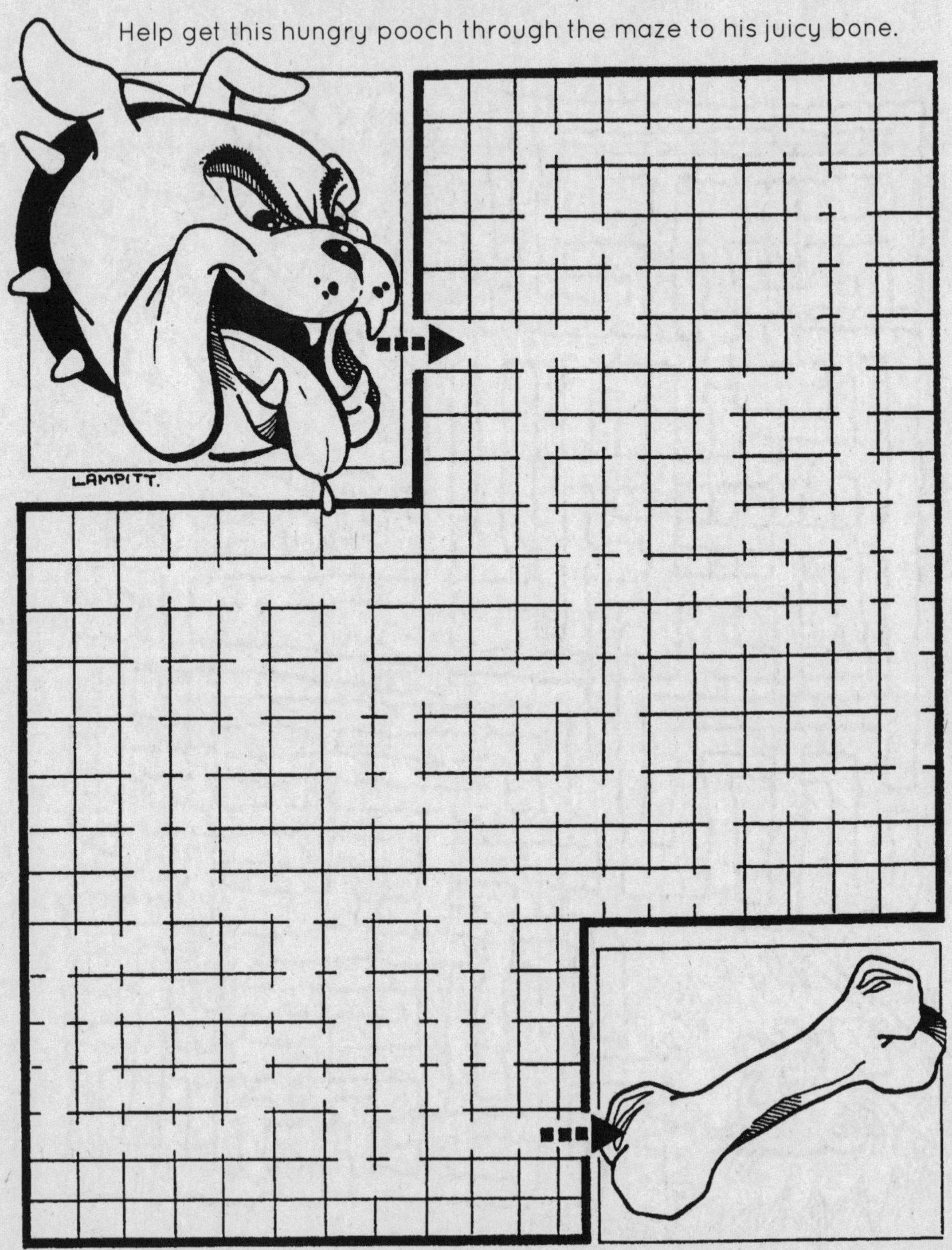

77
Note to Self

Can you follow a line from the note to the finish in one continuous movement?

78
Caveman Clues

Can you find the correct arrow trail to help this caveman get back to his cave?

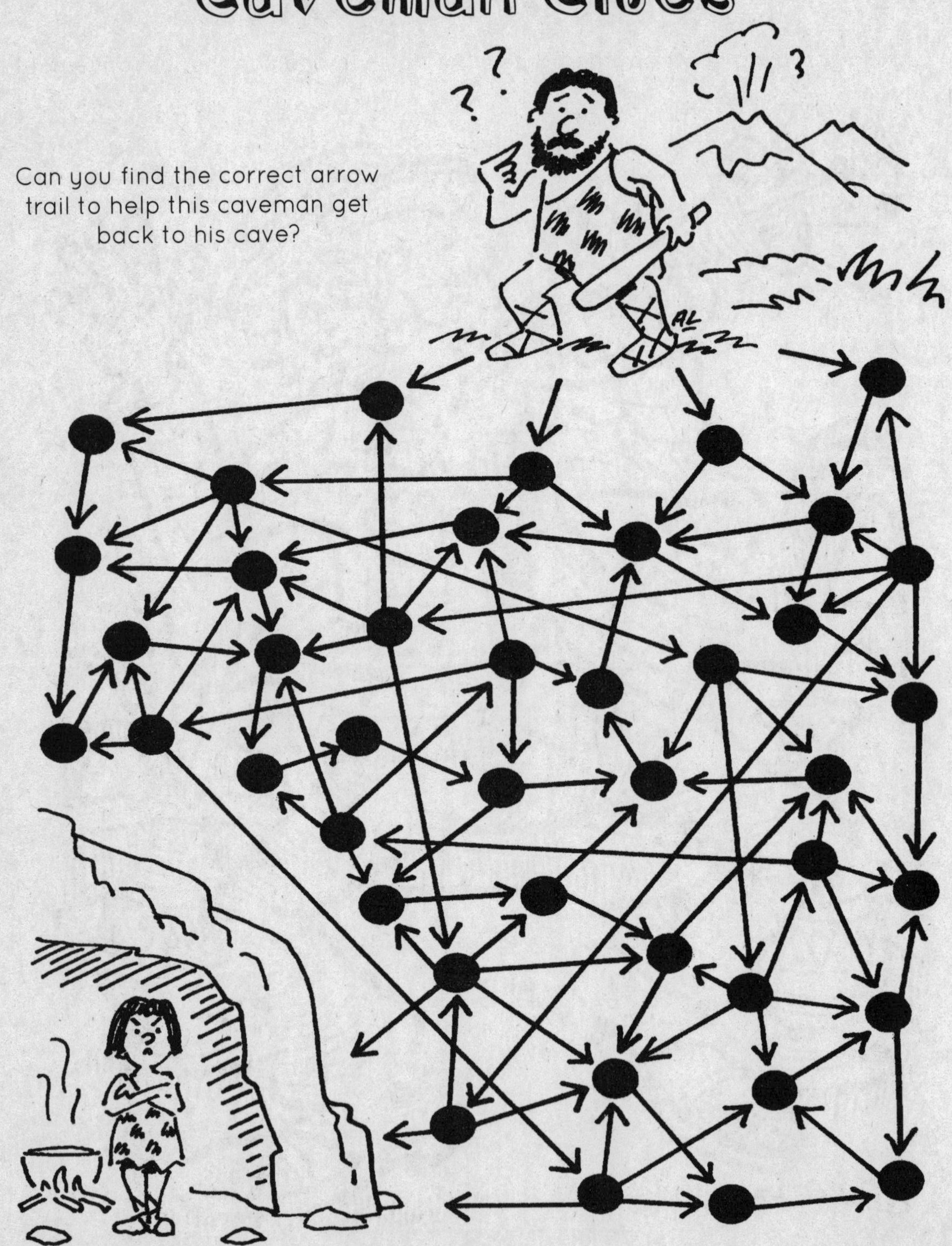

79

Sitting Pretty

Find your way from start to finish without crossing any solid lines.

Mouse Maze

Help this mouse get through the maze to his piece of cheese.

81

Back Pedal

Can you find the correct arrow trail to help this boy get back to the bag he's dropped?

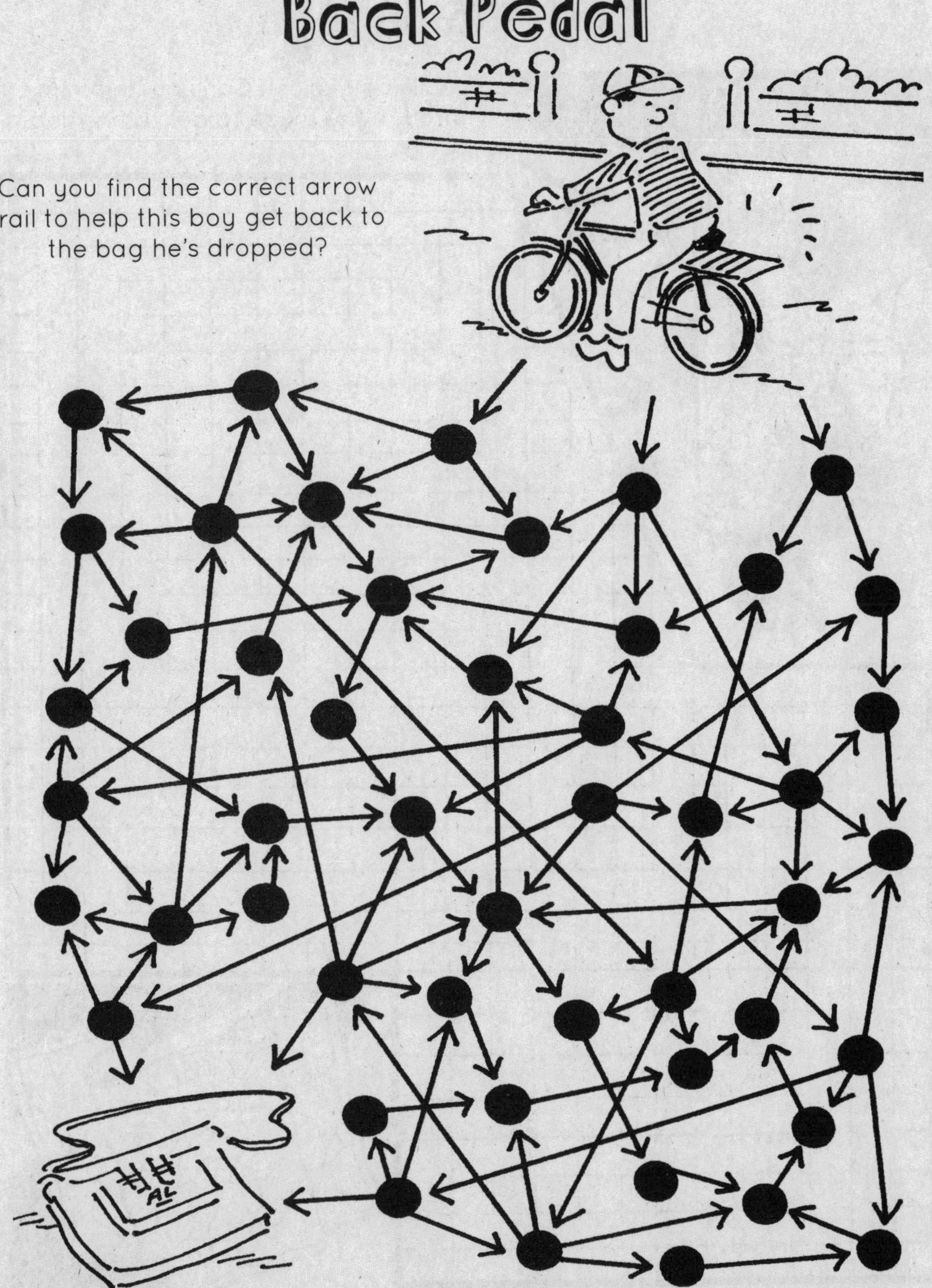

82

Route Map

This boy is lost. Can you help him through the maze to get to his map?

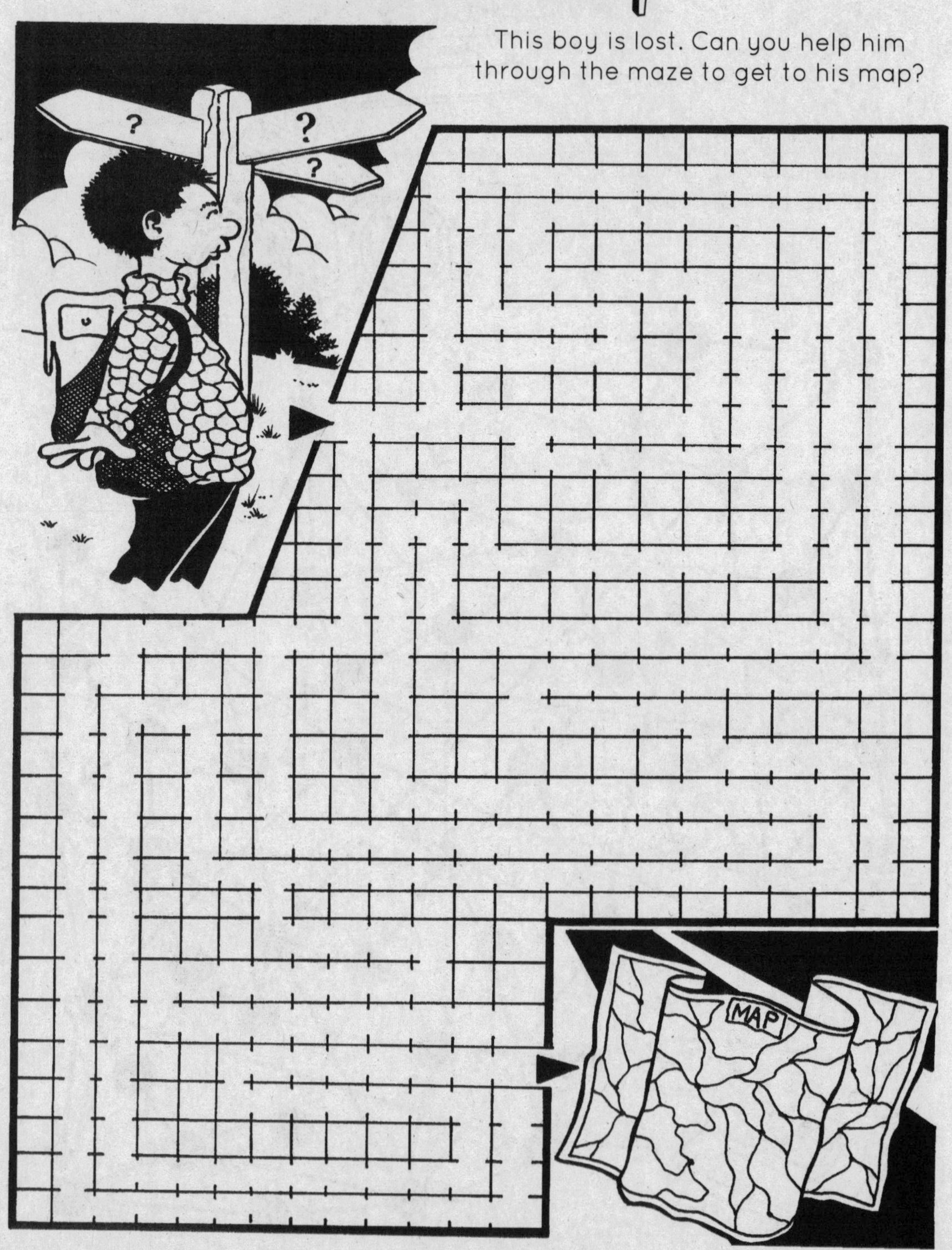

83

Homeward Bound

Help get these kids home and avoid the witch.

84

Arrow Trail

Can you find the correct arrow trail to get the arrow to the target and avoid the greenhouse?

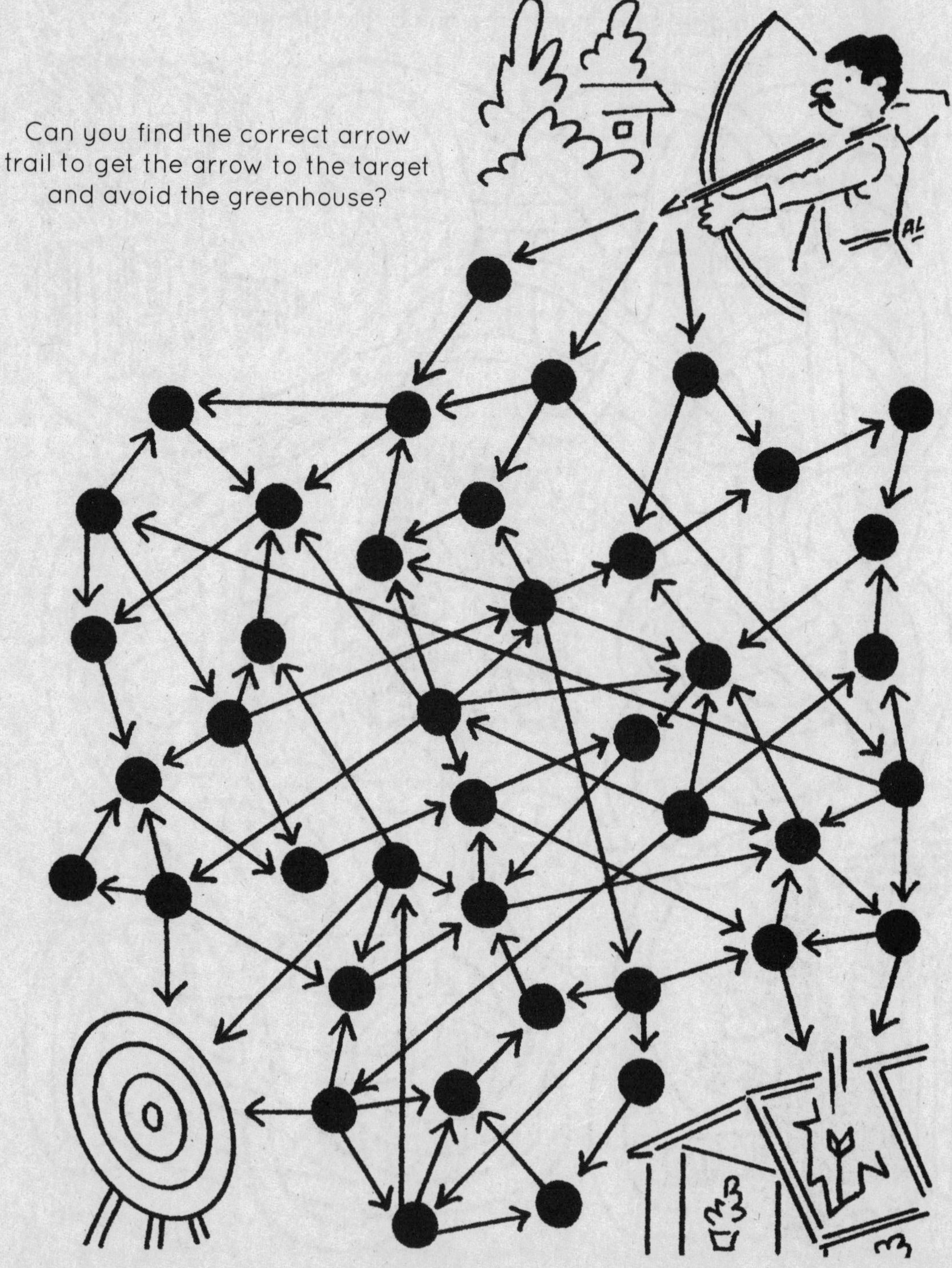

85

Glove Story

Help this mouse find a path to his other boxing glove.

86

Polar Problem

Find your way from start to finish without crossing any solid lines.

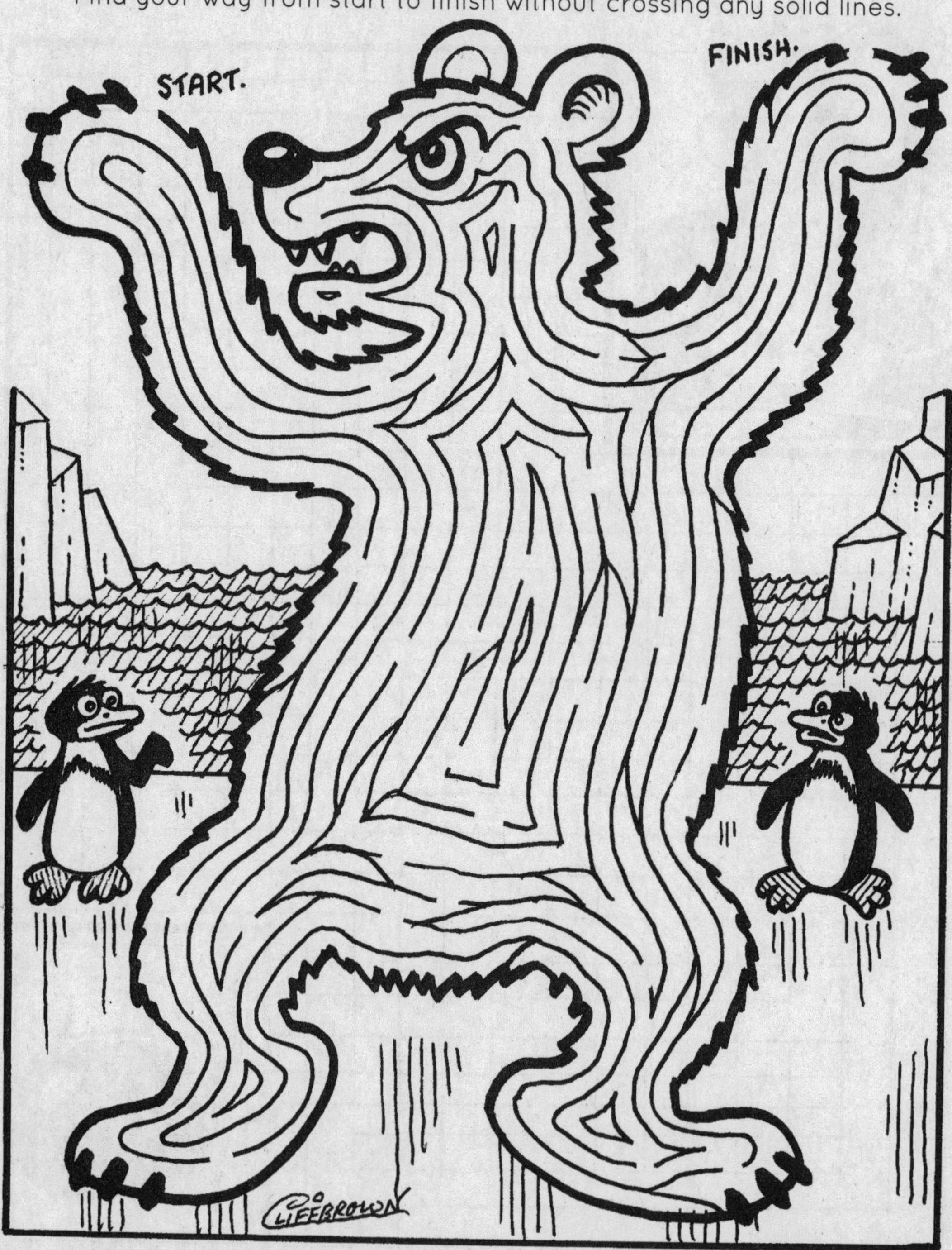

87

Up, Up, and Away!

Can you find the correct arrow trail to get this boy back down to Earth?

88

From Head to Tail

Find your way from start to finish without crossing any solid lines.

89

Brush Up

See if you can find a way through the maze to get to the toothpaste.

90

Treasure Map

Can you find the correct arrow trail to get this pirate to the treasure and avoid the alligator?

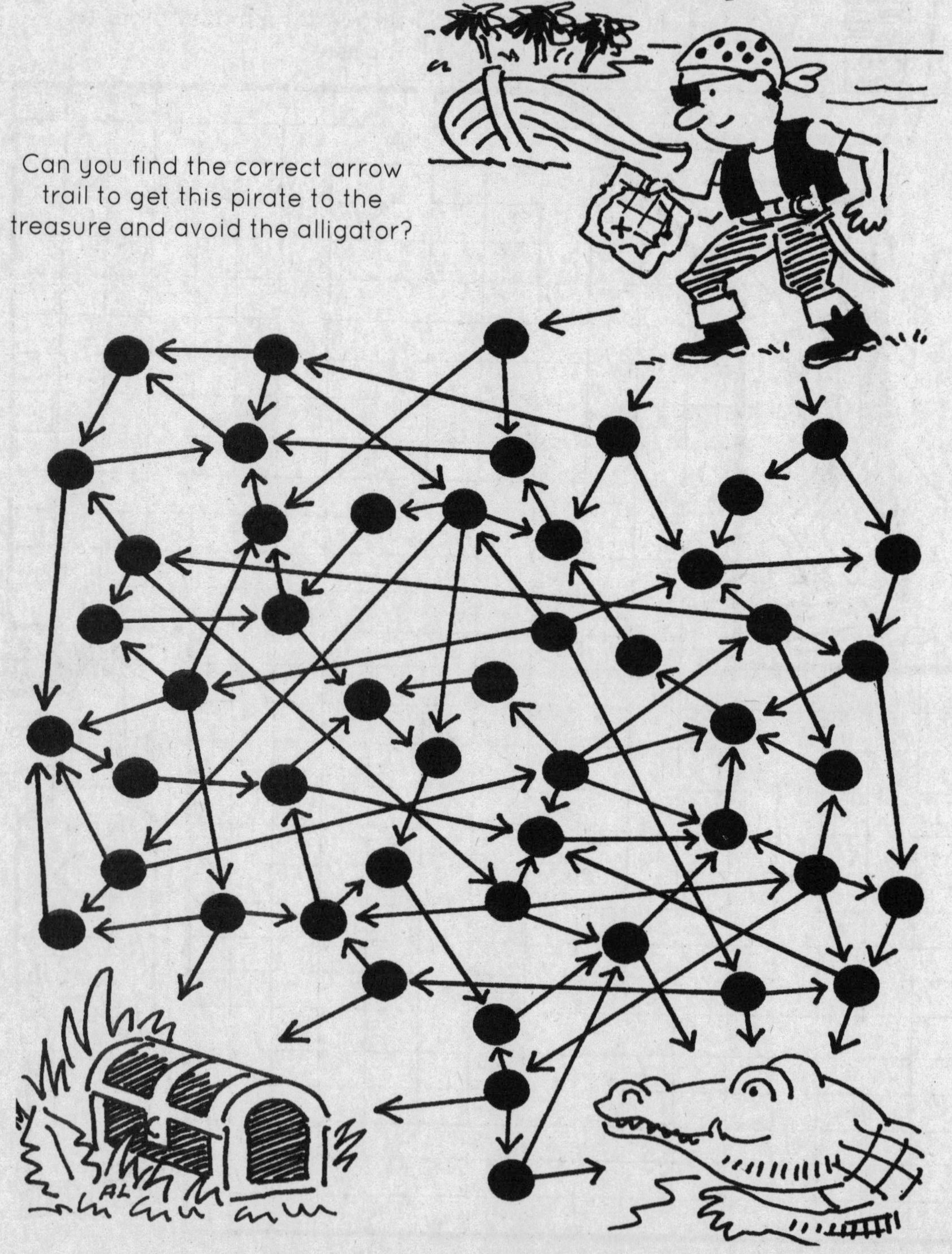

Outer Space

Can you find a way through the maze from the telescope to the planet?

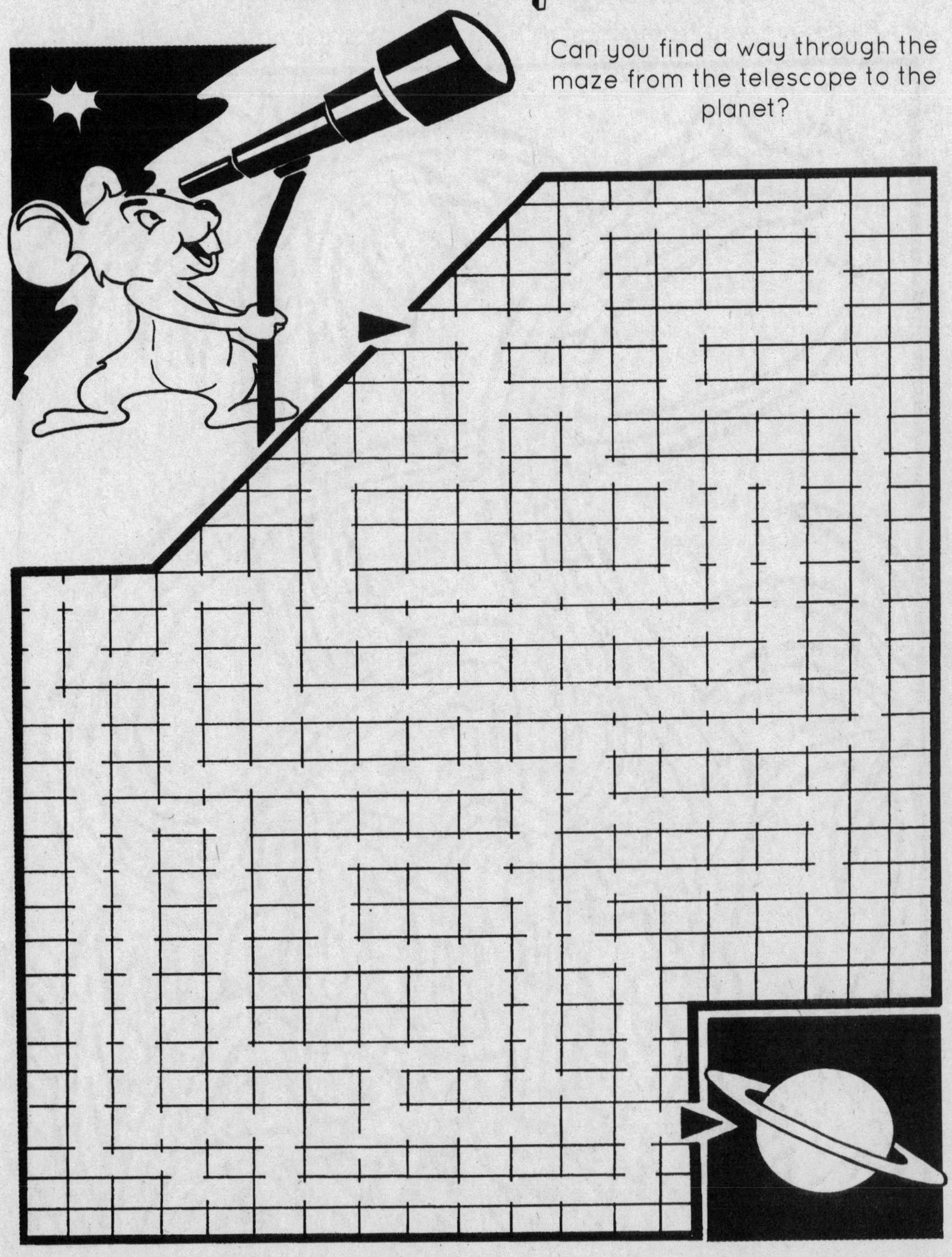

Jurassic Path

Find your way from start to finish without crossing any solid lines.

93
Desert Drinks

Can you find the correct arrow trail to get this man to the oasis and avoid the mirage?

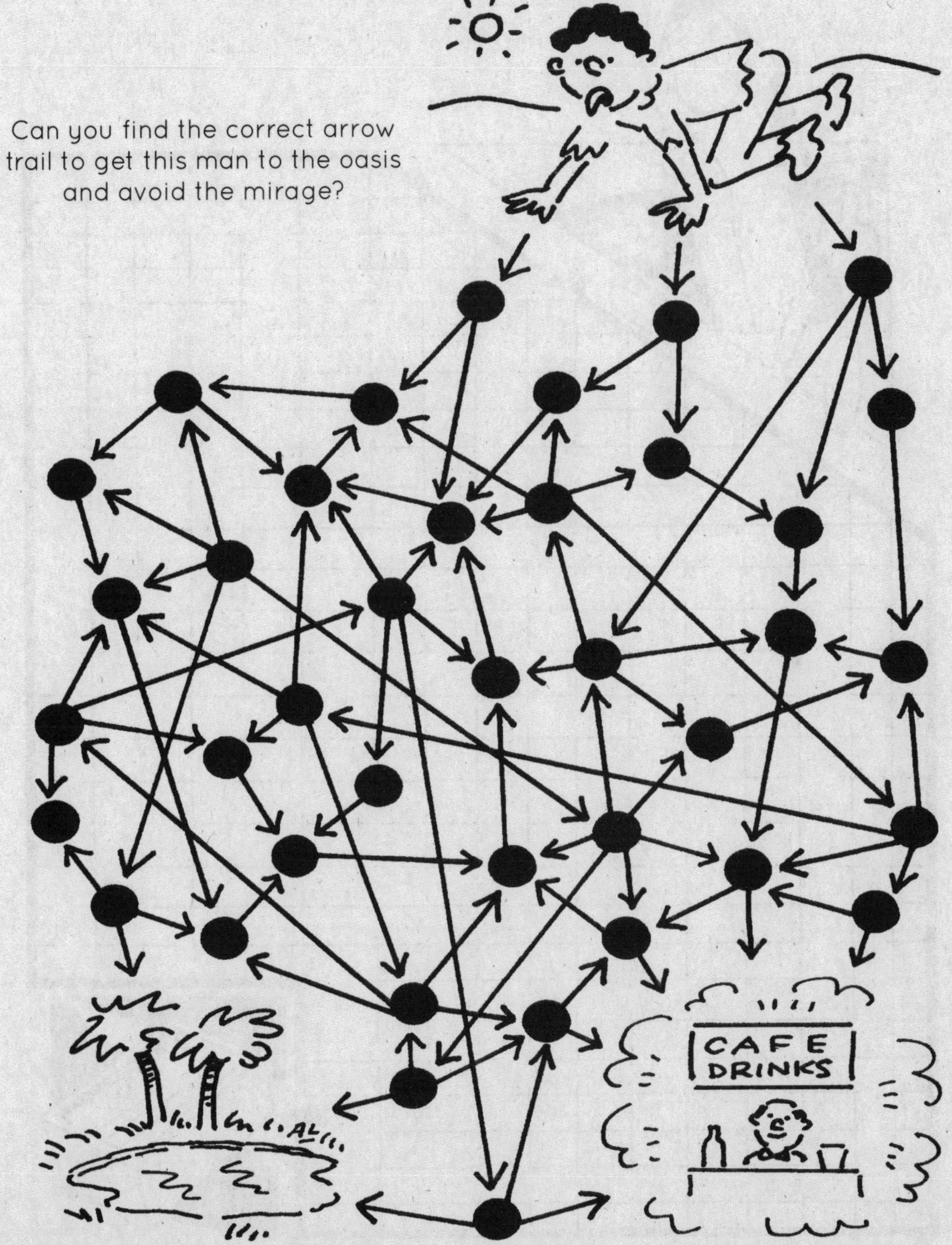

94

Pencil Path

Help this pencil get to the sharpener.

95

Alien Sighting

Find your way from start to finish without crossing any solid lines.

96

Bounce to It

Can you find the correct arrow trail to get this kangaroo back to his mother?

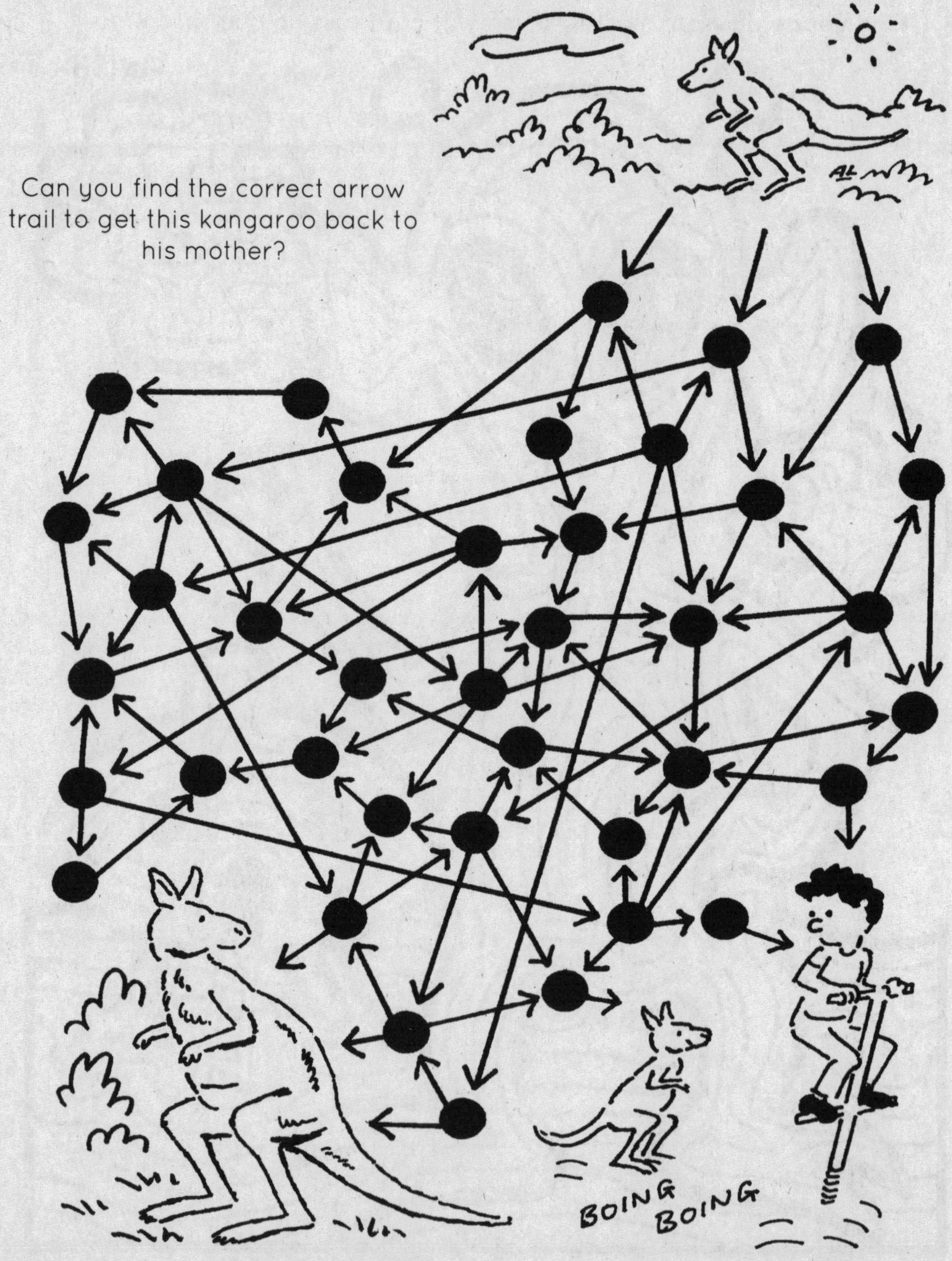

97

Dig It

Find a path through the maze to get to the broken part of the spade.

98
Bee Happy

Can you find a path through this maze so the bee goes to collect pollen and then back to the hive?

99
A Place in Space

Can you find the correct arrow trail to help this rocket get to the planet and avoid getting stuck on its rings?

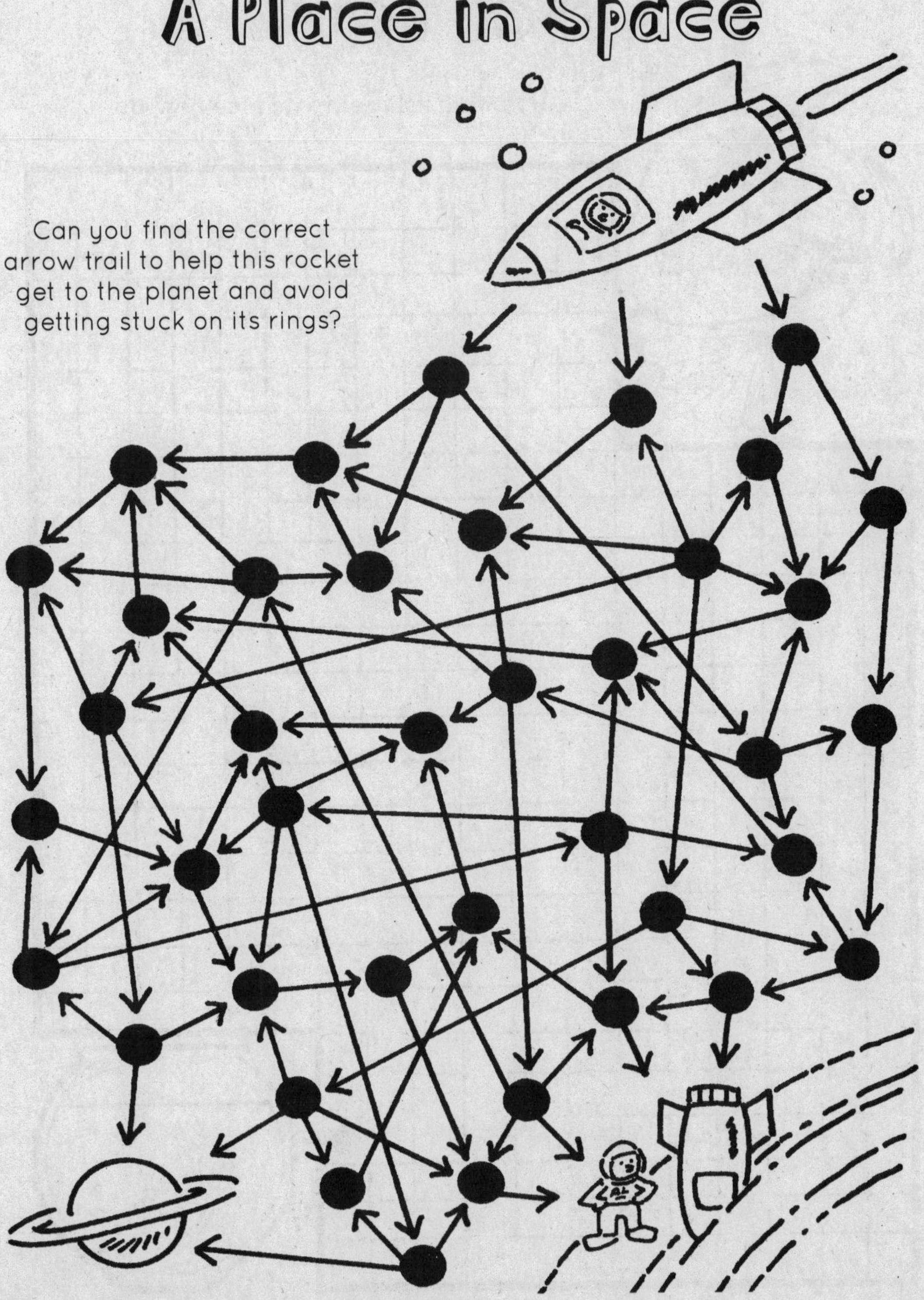

Super Bowl

Help this fish get to its nice new bowl.

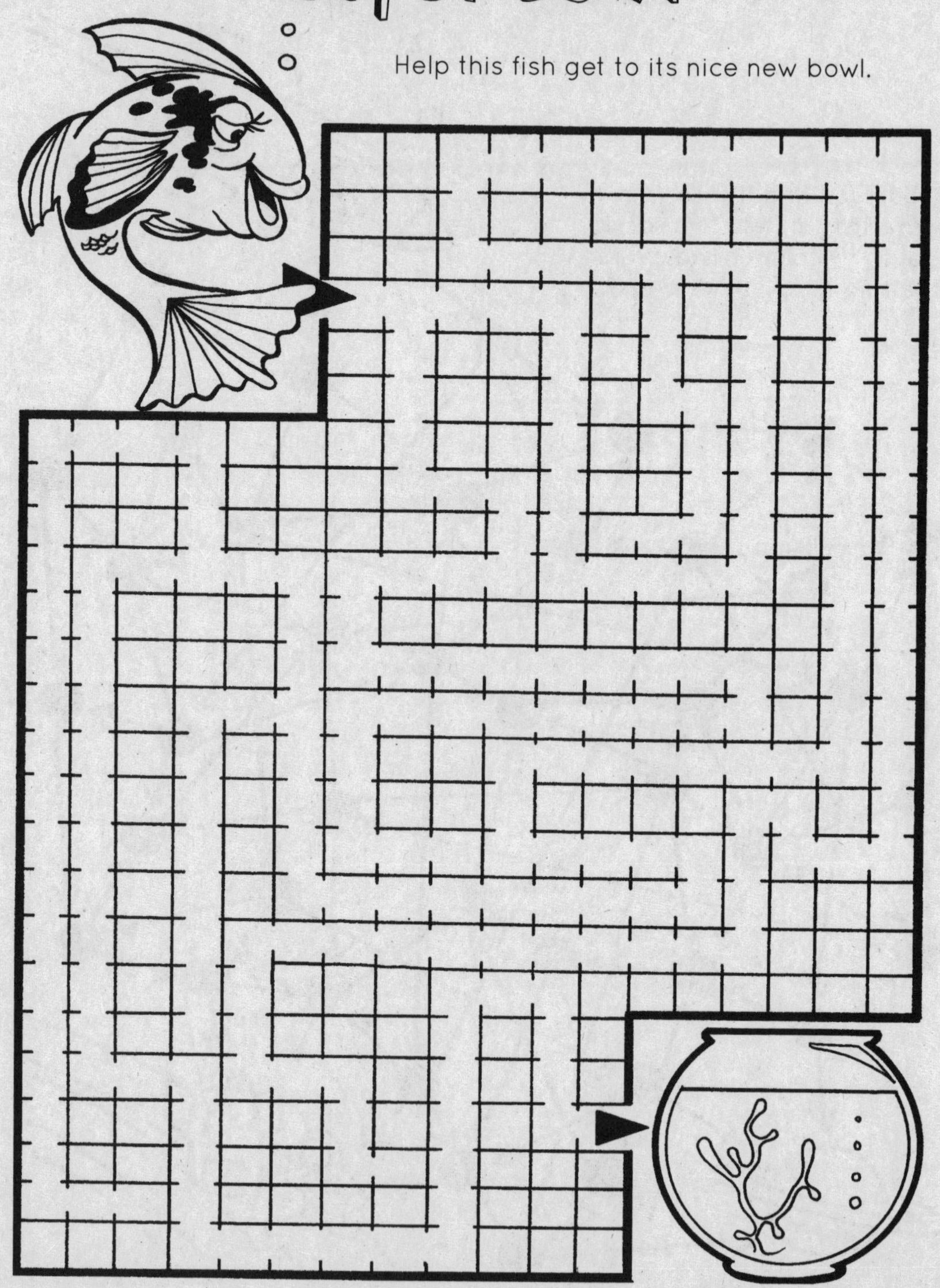

101

Going Bananas

Only one of these monkeys will get to the banana. Can you work out which one it is?

102

Brick by Brick

See if you can guide this man back to finish building the wall.

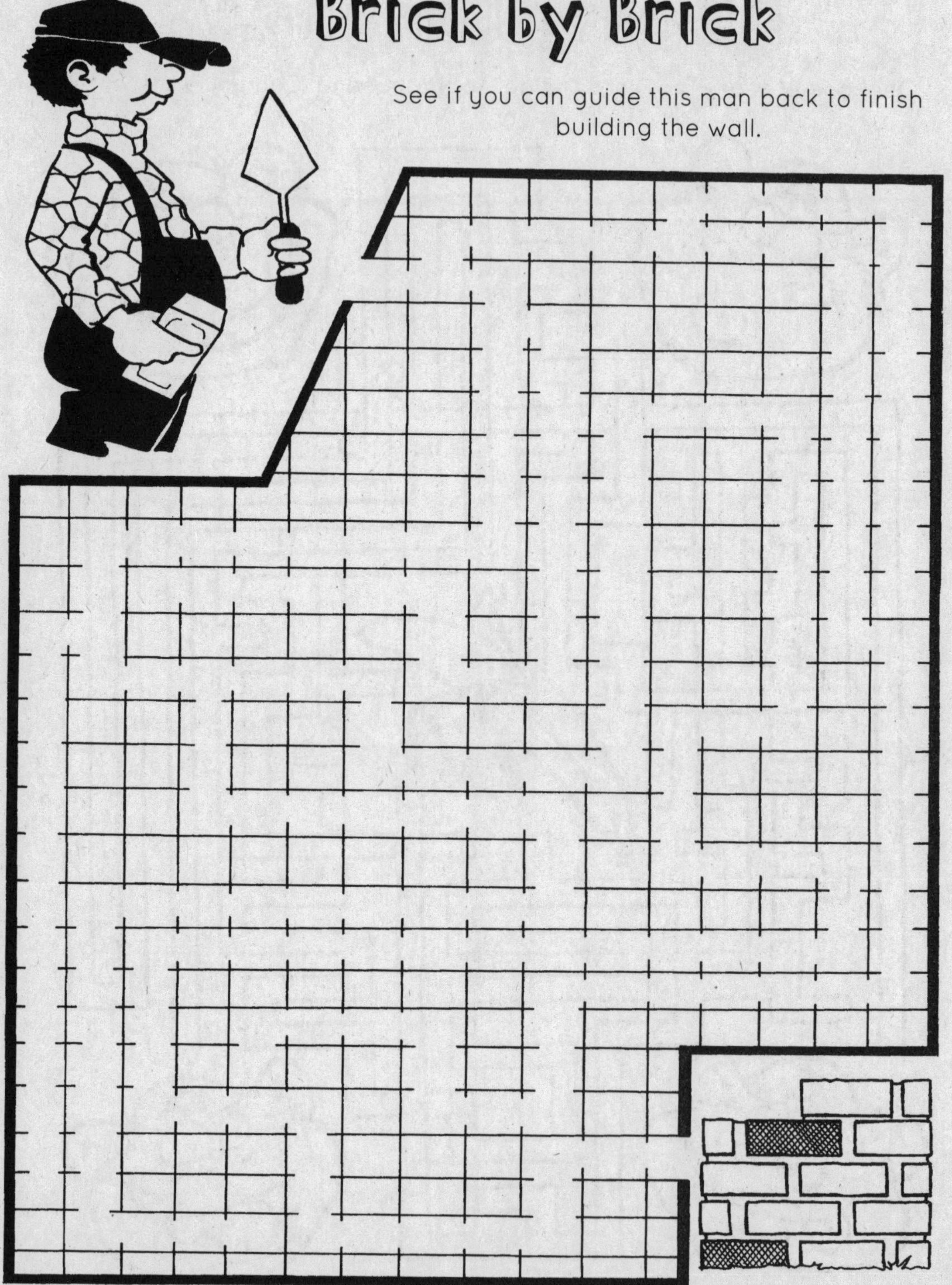

103

Bird Brain

Help this bird get to the egg that's fallen out of her nest.

104

Caveman Trail

Can you find the correct arrow trail to help UG get back to his cave?

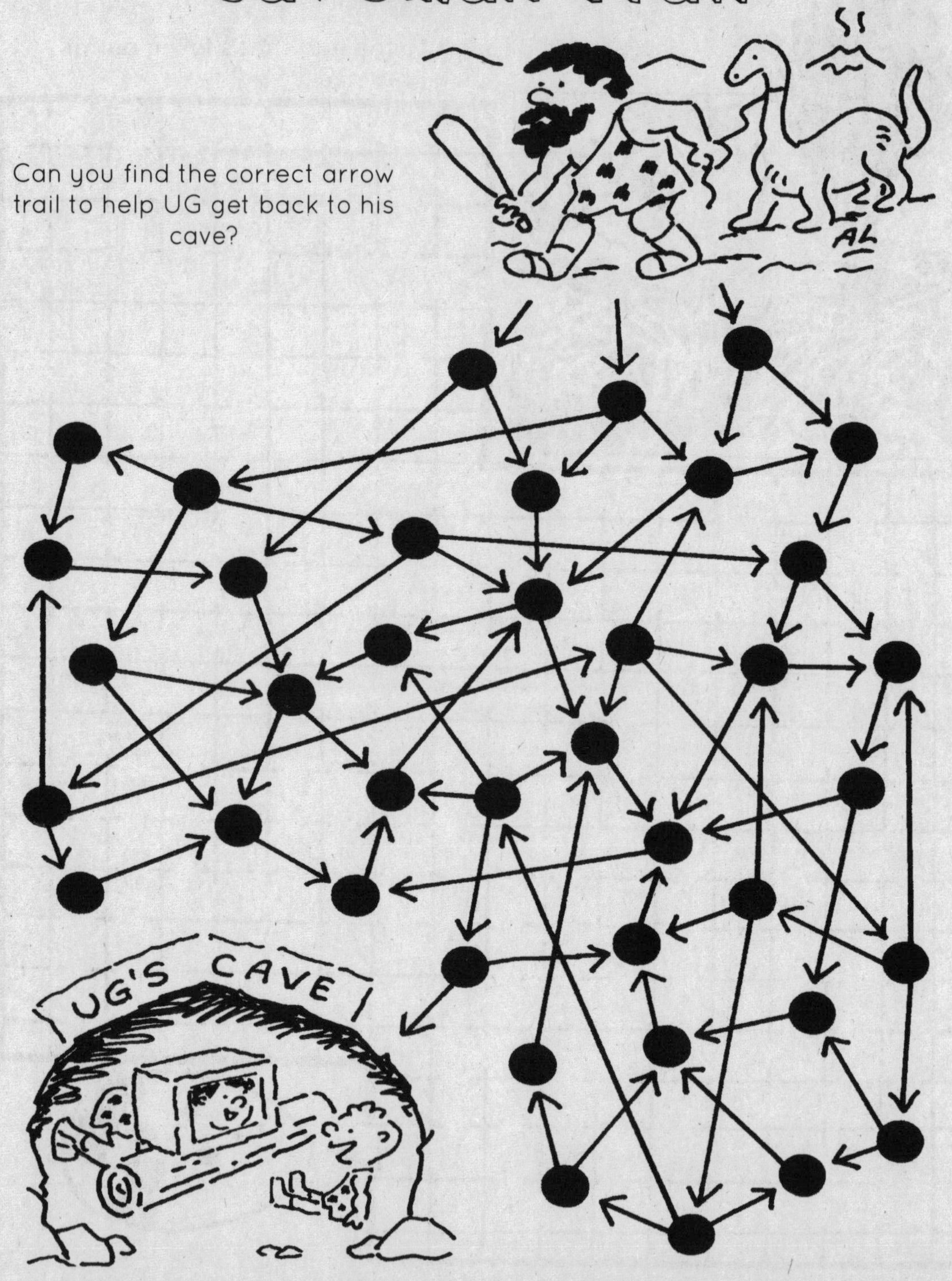

105

Rabbit Run

Help this rabbit get to the tasty vegetables and avoid the wolf.

106

UFO Search

Try to help this alien find his way back to his flying saucer.

107

Statue Path

Find your way from start to finish on this statue without crossing any solid lines.

108
Horse Race

Can you find the correct arrow trail to help this rider get to the finish line and avoid falling in the water?

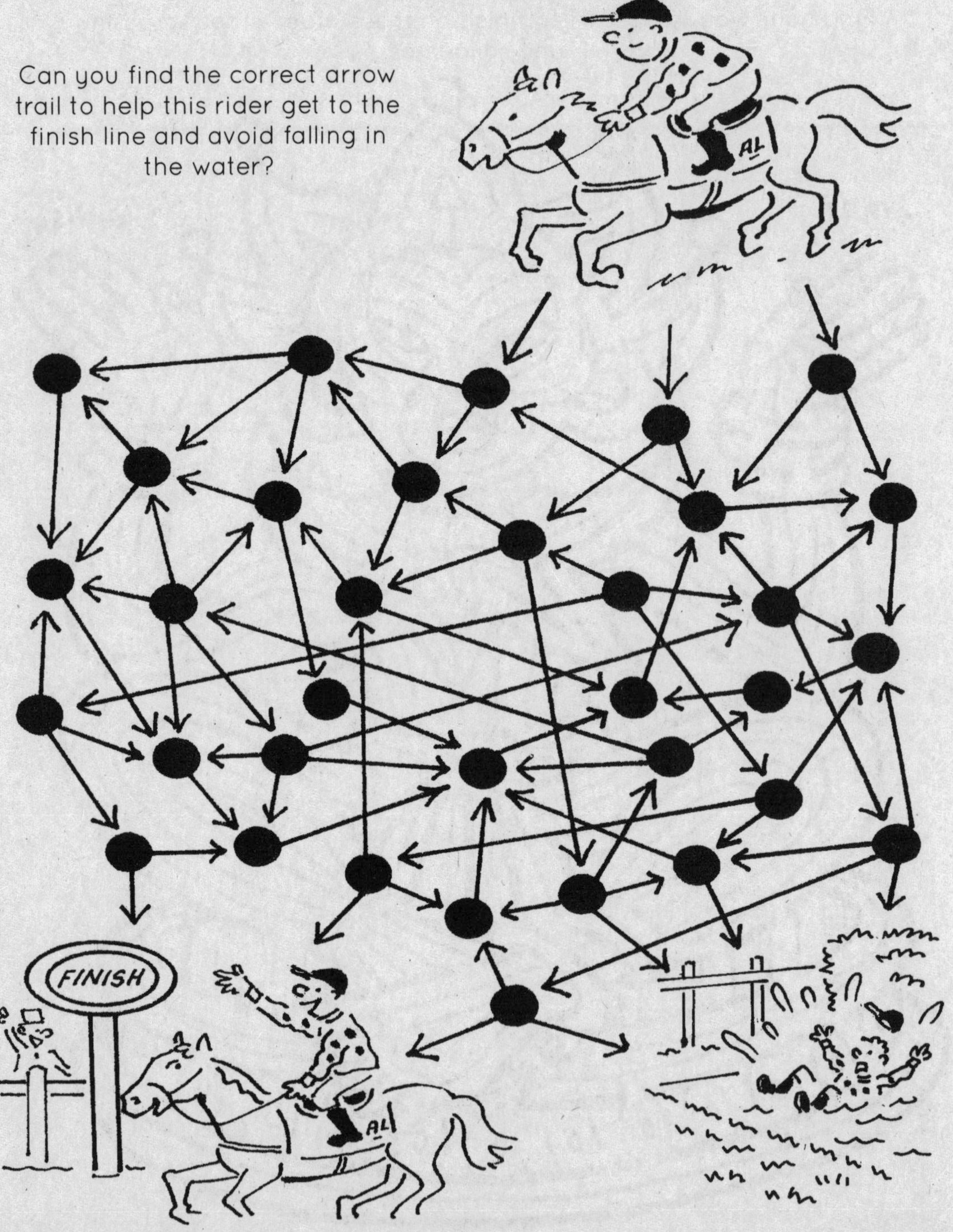

109

Painted Lines

Can you help this paint can through the maze to get to the brush?

110

Hole in One

Help this golfer through the maze to the hole avoiding the bunkers.

111

Comfy Seat

Which path should this stool take to get to its cushion?

112

Kick Off

Can you find the correct arrow trail to help this soccer player hit the net and not smash the window?

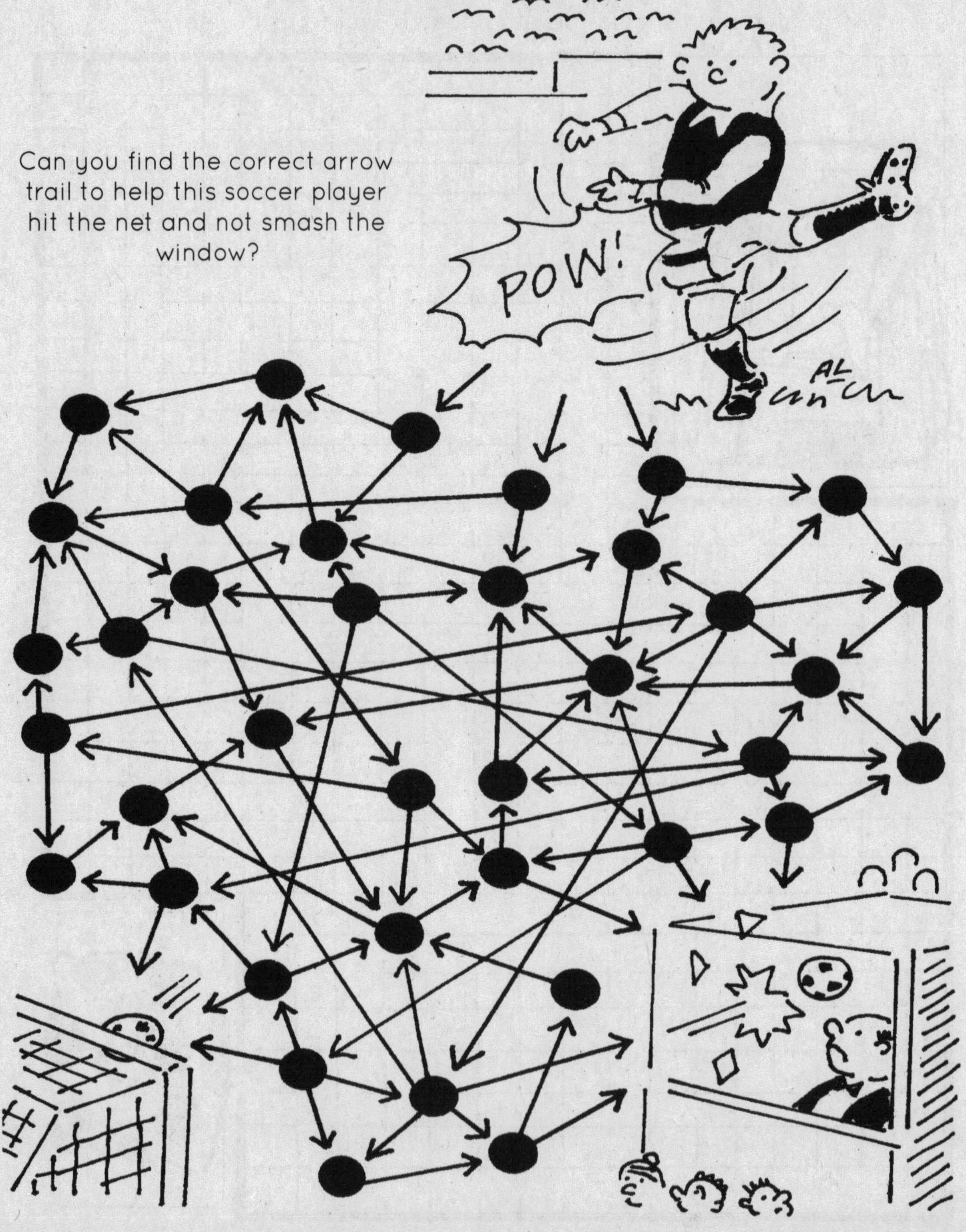

113

Jumbo Puzzle

Find your way from start to finish without crossing any solid lines.

114
Rabbit Food

See if you can find a path through the maze to get to the vegetables.

115
Drop Zone

Help this man land safely and avoid all the hazards.

116

Abracadabra

Can you find the correct arrow trail to help this magician make the woman disappear and not his magic wand?

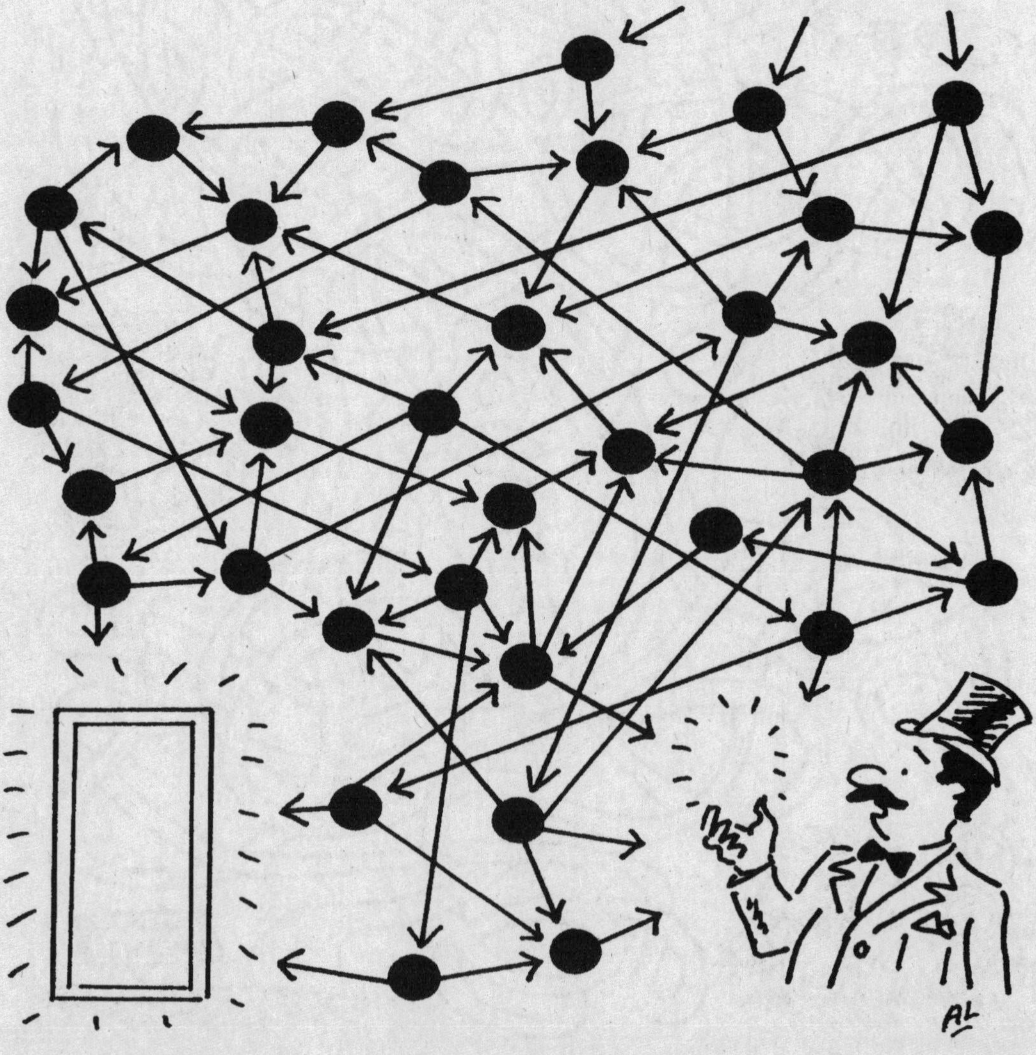

Water, Water Everywhere

Find a path through the maze to get the water to the flower.

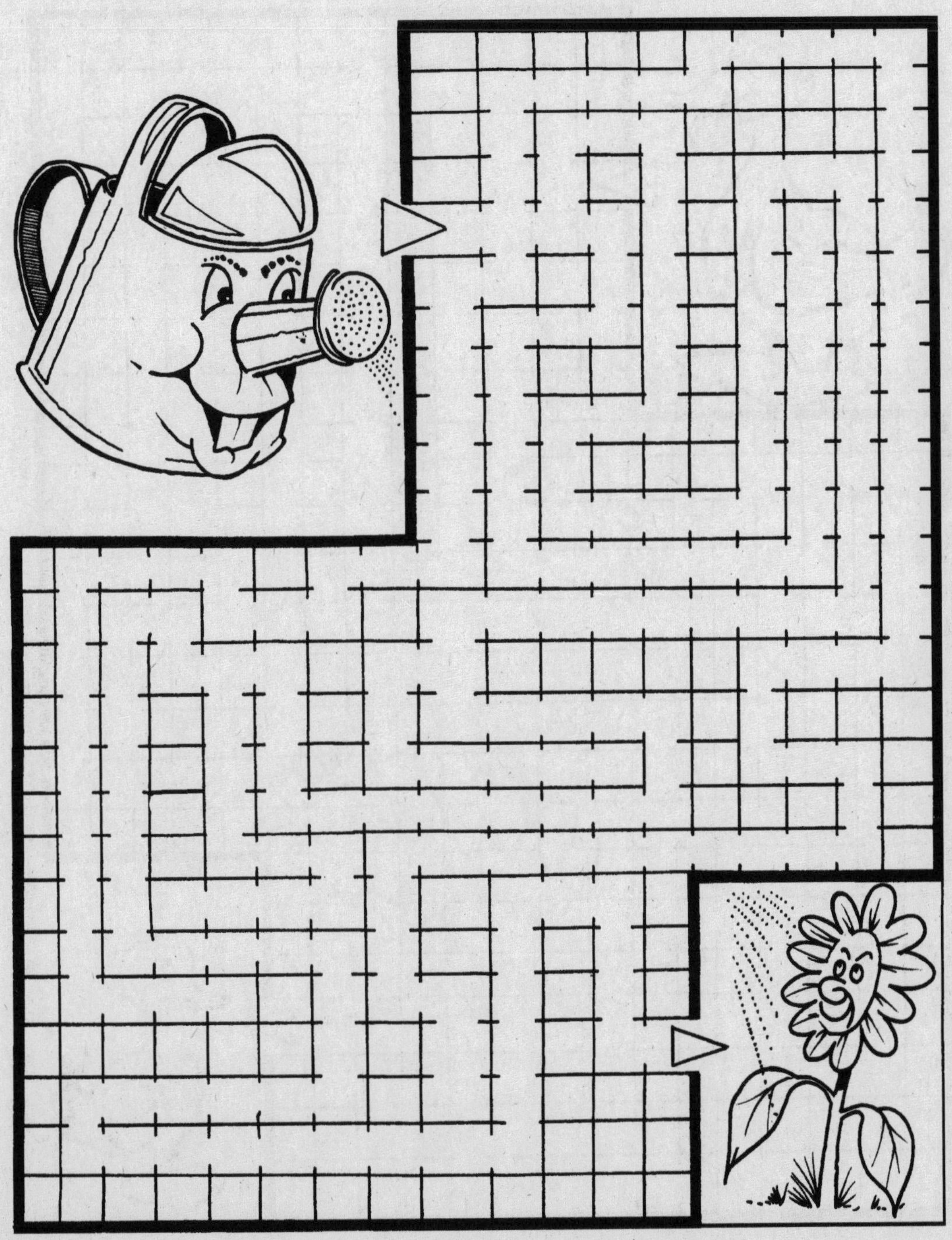

118

Quackers

Help this mother duck through the maze to her duckling.

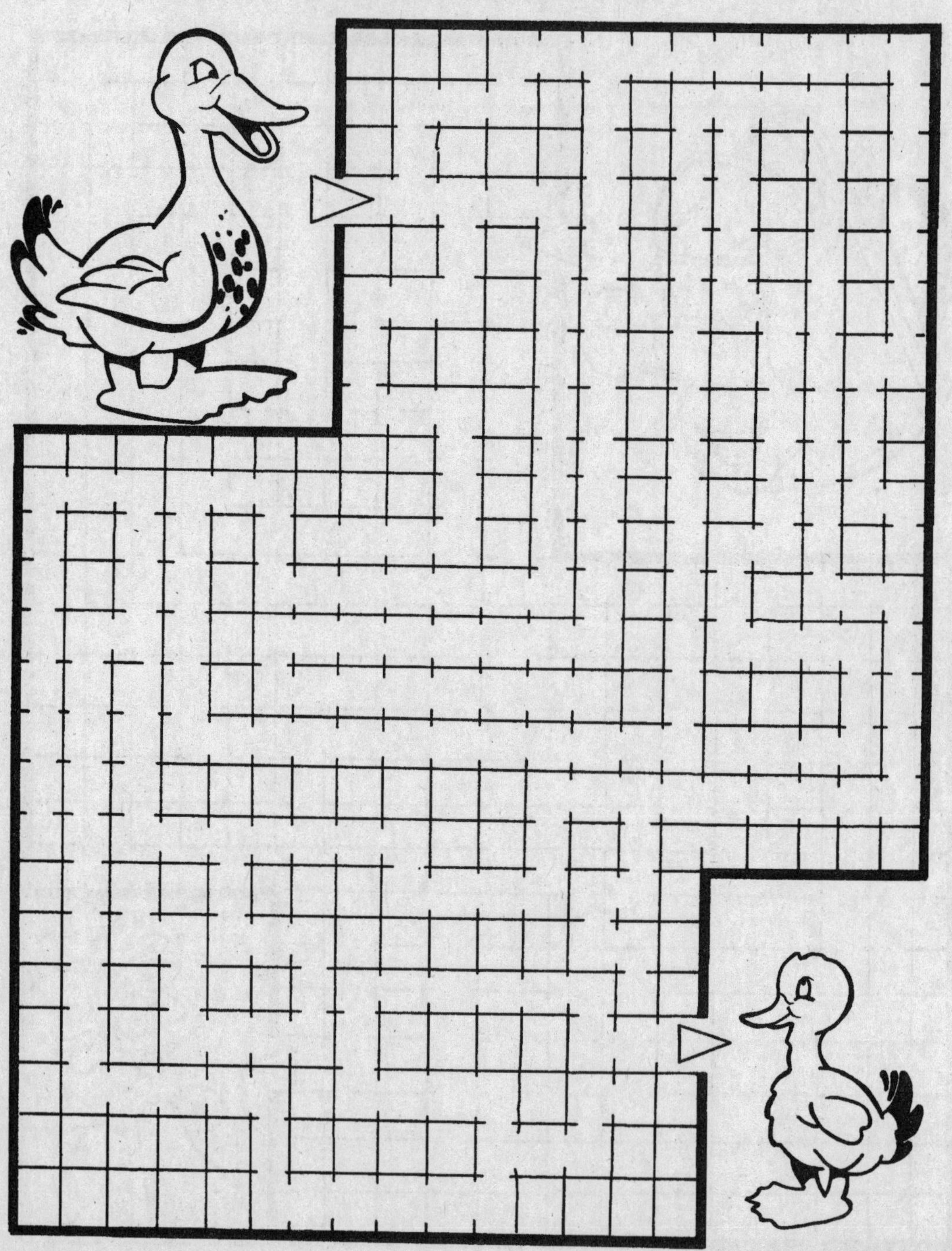

119

Going Shopping

This boy needs to get to the shop and back to where he started. Can you help him out?

120
Bull in a China Shop

Can you find the correct arrow trail to help the bull get to the bullfighter and avoid the china shop?

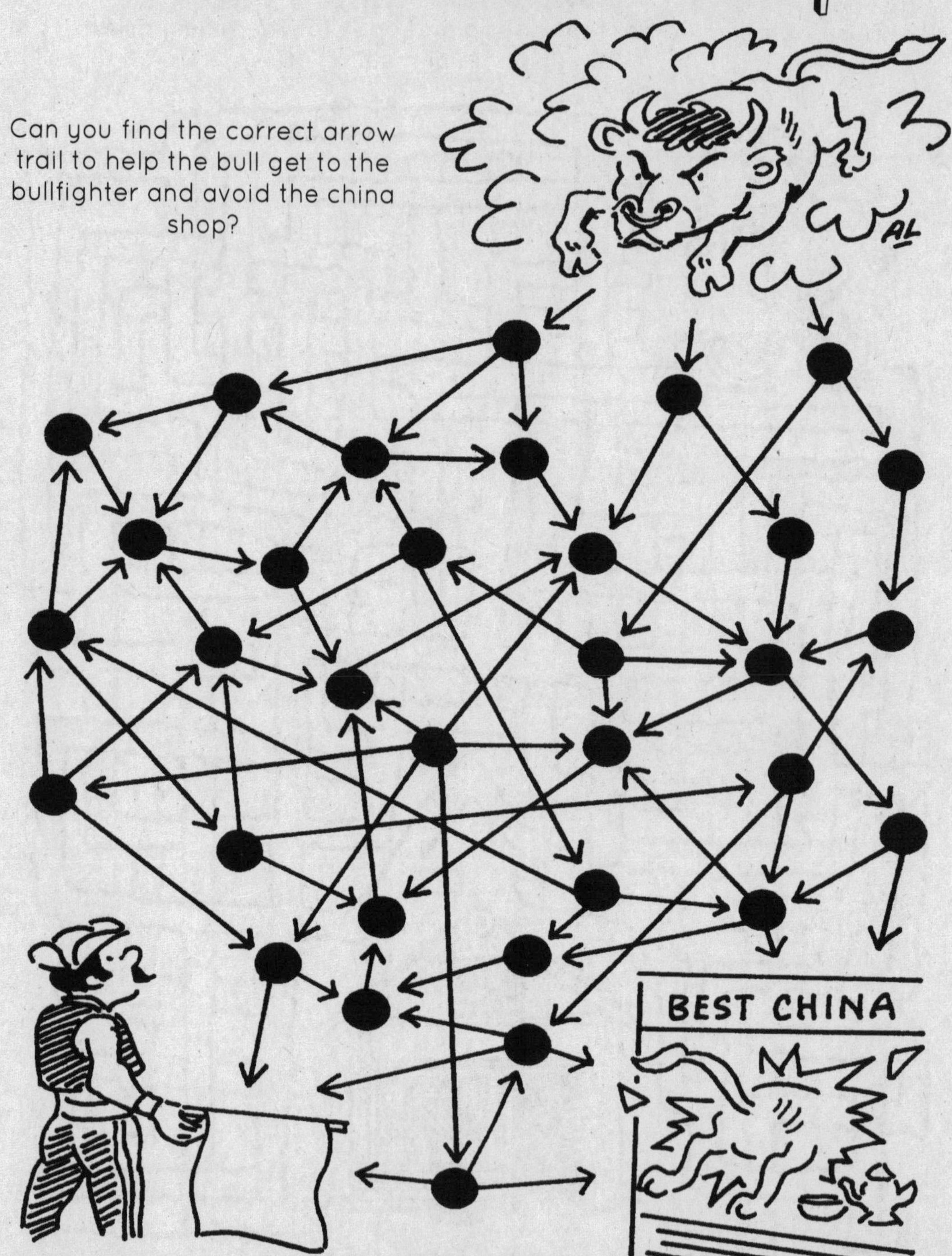

121

Donkey Path

Find a path through the maze to help the donkey get his carrot.

122

Dragon Maze

Find your way from start to finish without crossing any solid lines.

123

Late for the Match

Can you find the correct arrow trail to help this soccer player get to the stadium and avoid the crowd of fans?

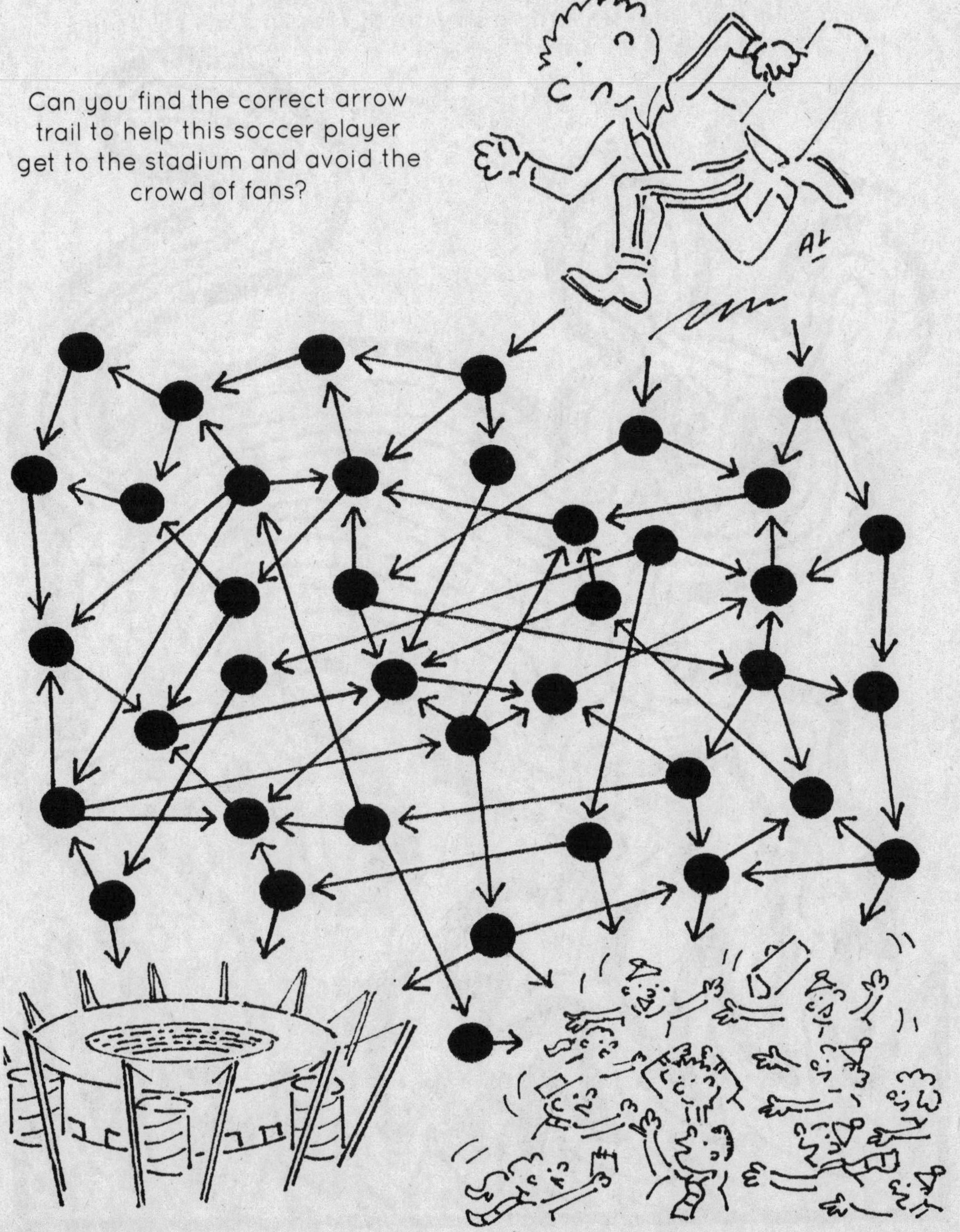

124
Lamb Lines

Find your way from start to finish without crossing any solid lines.

125

Heads or Tails

Can you find the correct arrow trail to help the referee get to the coin before the dog runs off with it?

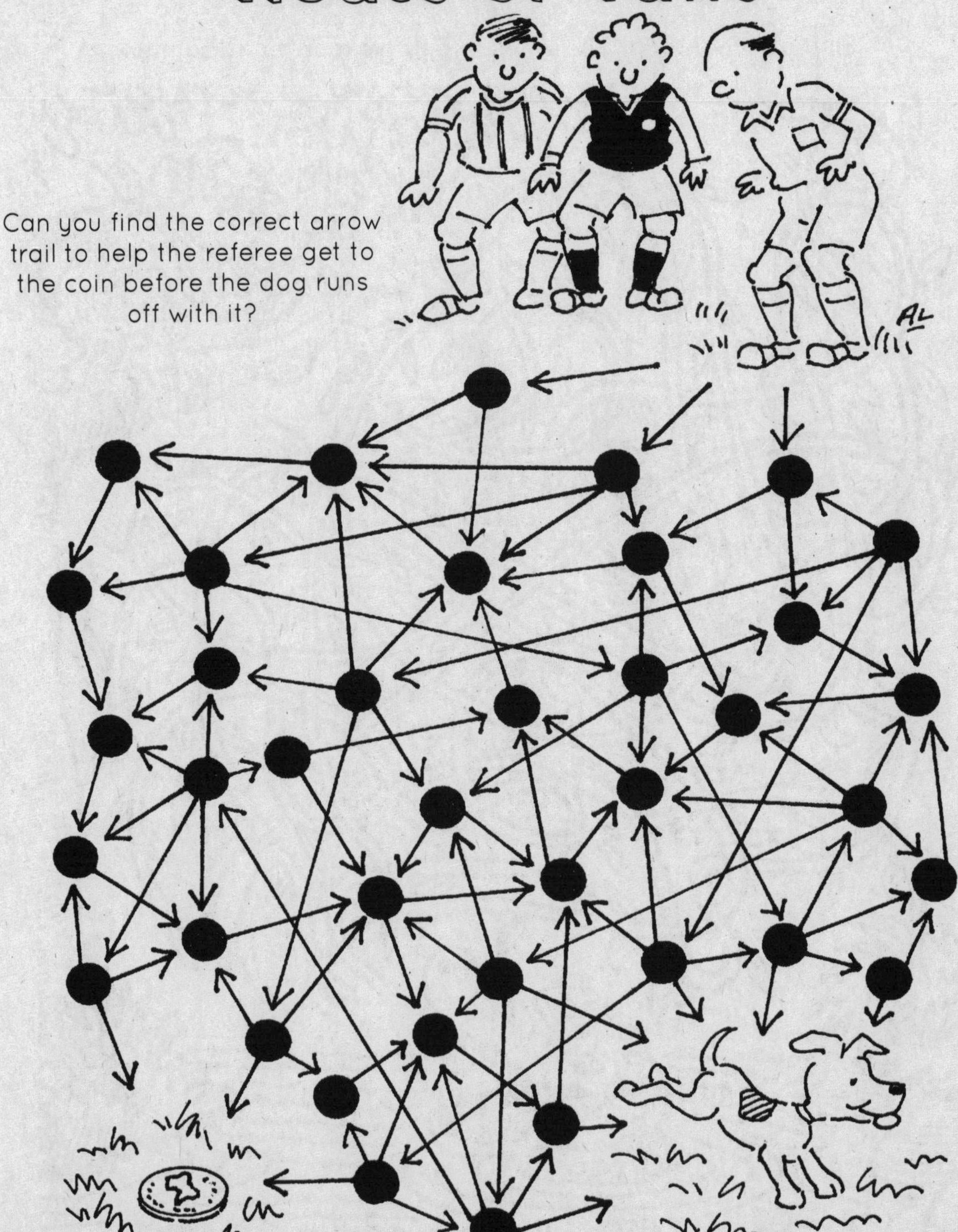

126

Monkey Maze

Find a path through the vines to get this monkey to safety.

127
Goat Path

Find your way from start to finish without crossing any solid lines.

128
Cross the Street

Can you find the correct arrow trail to help this boy get to the road crossing and avoid going to the zoo?

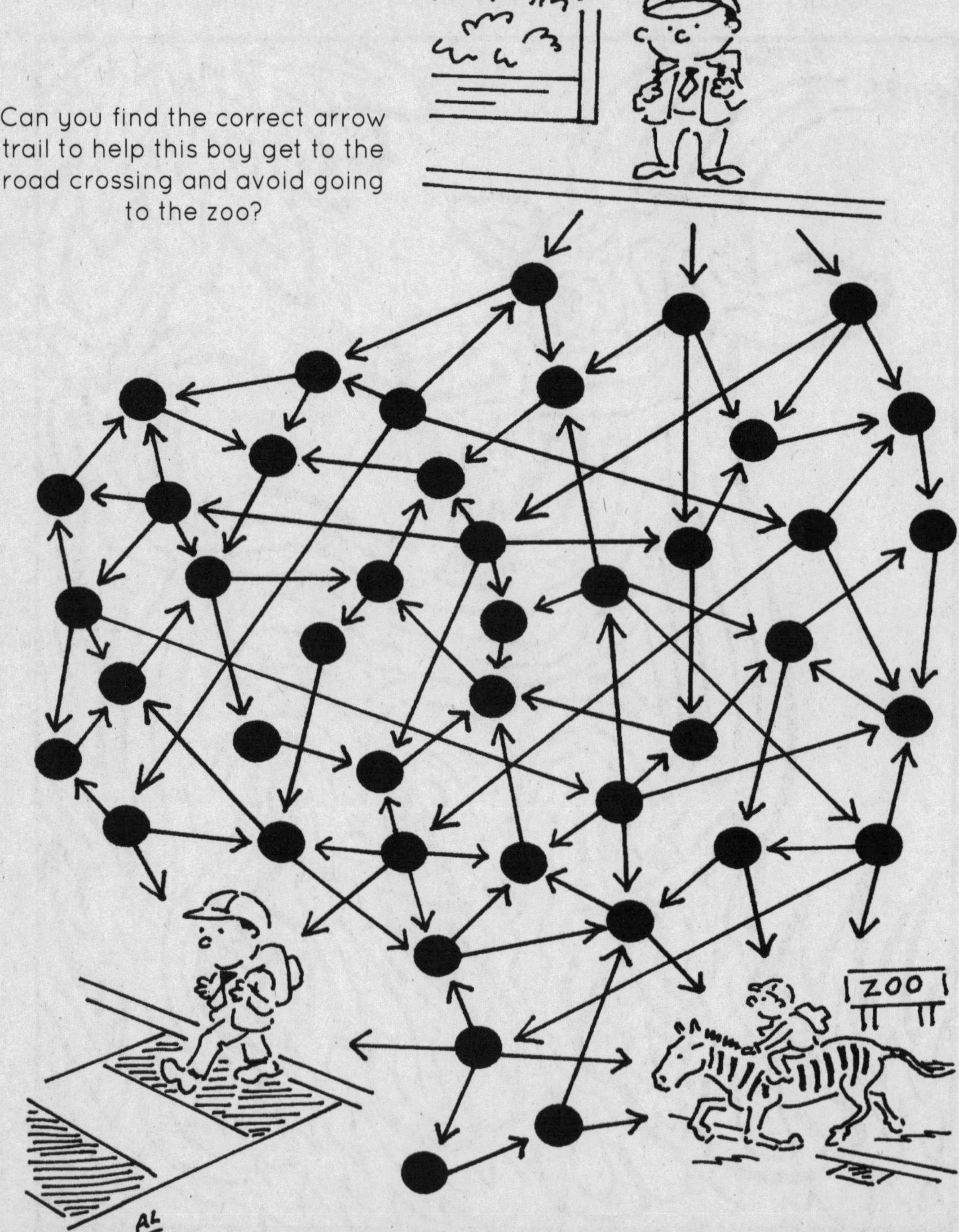

Solutions

1

2

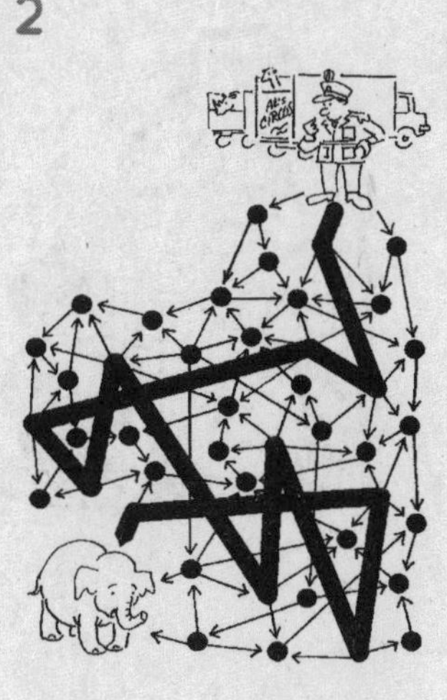

3

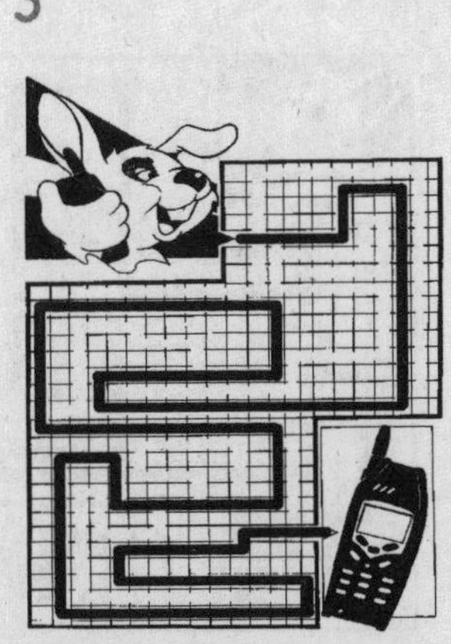

4

5

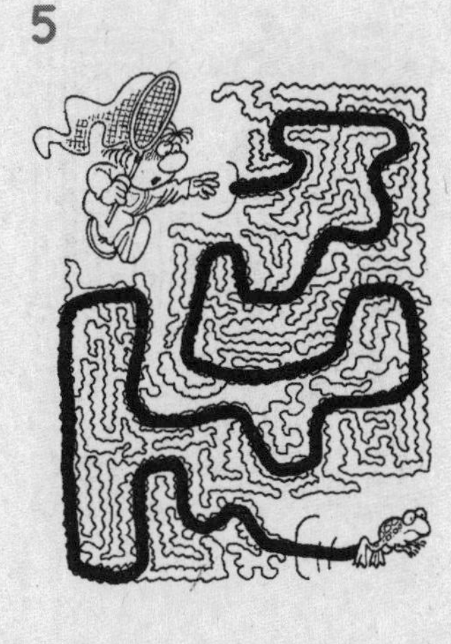

6

7

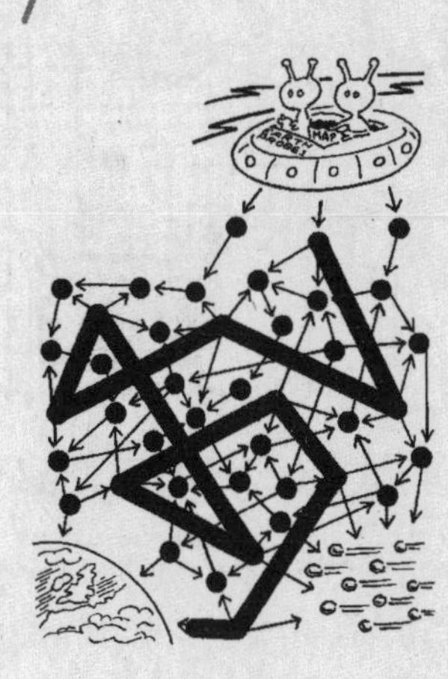

8

9

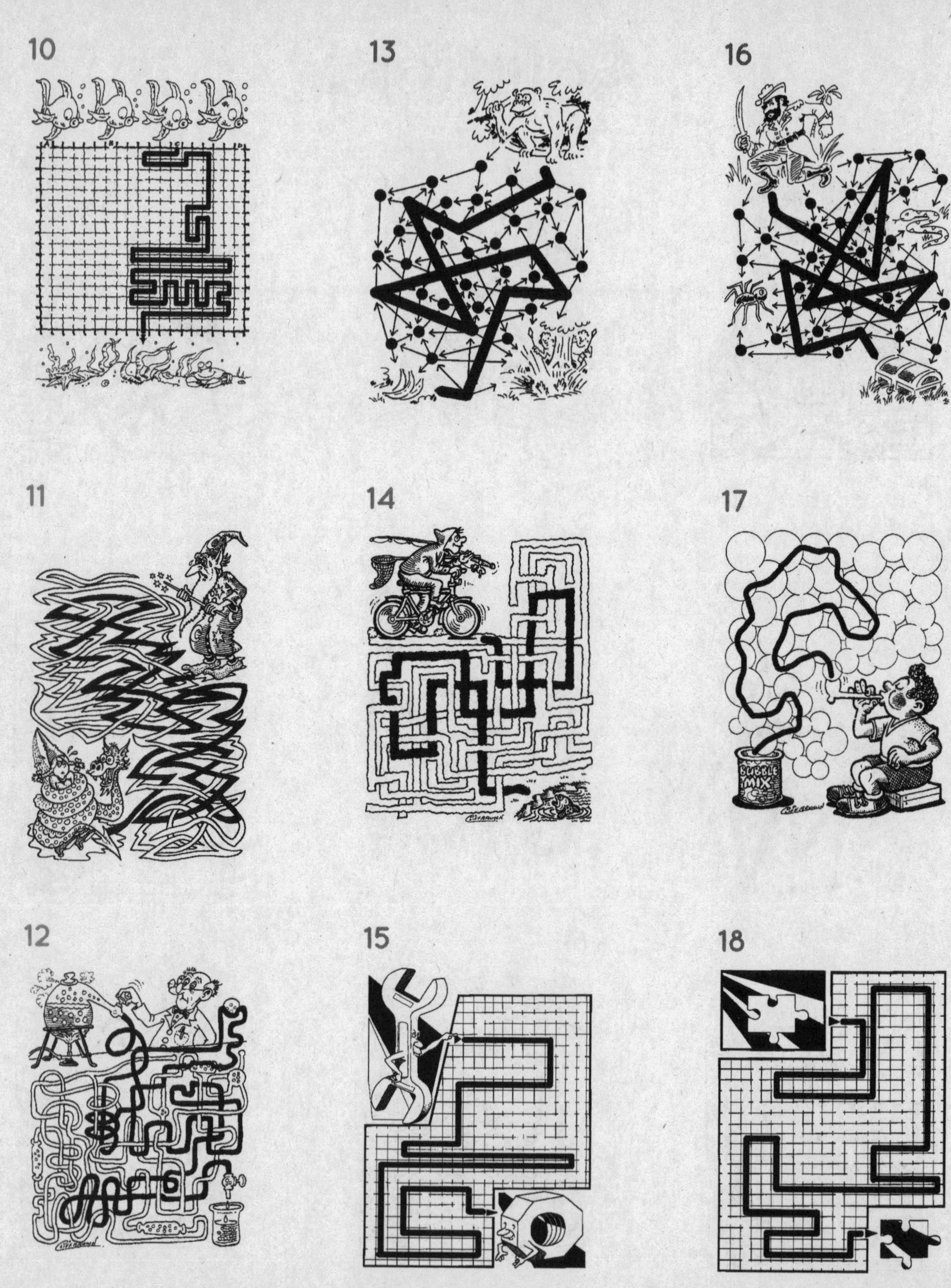
10
13
16
11
14
17
BUBBLE MIX
12
15
18

19

20

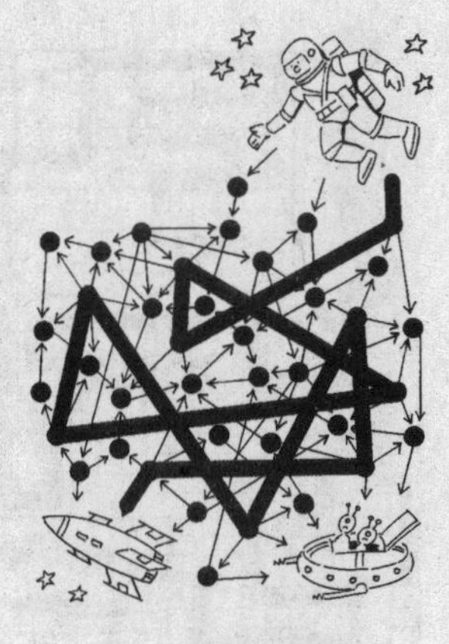

21

22

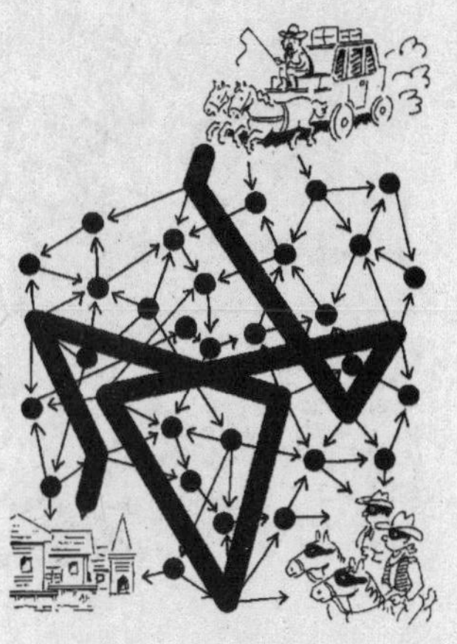

23

24

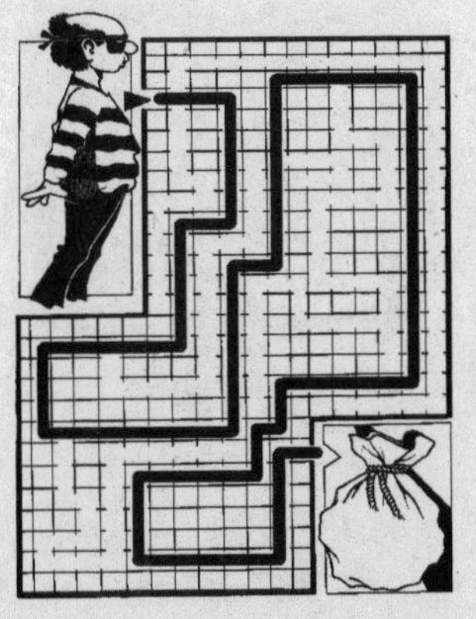

25

26

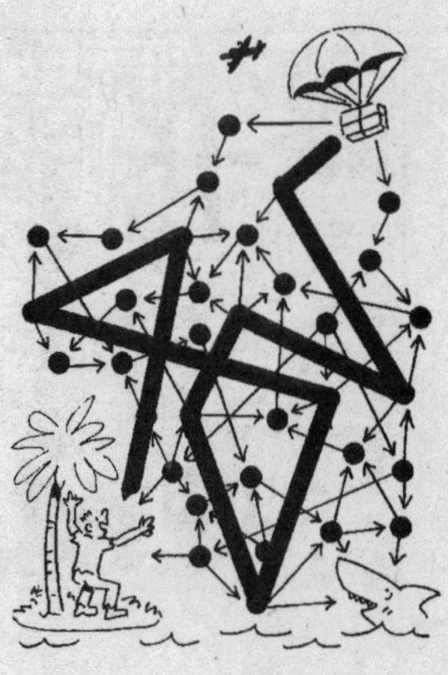

27

28

29

YE OLDE LOST ... MINE

30

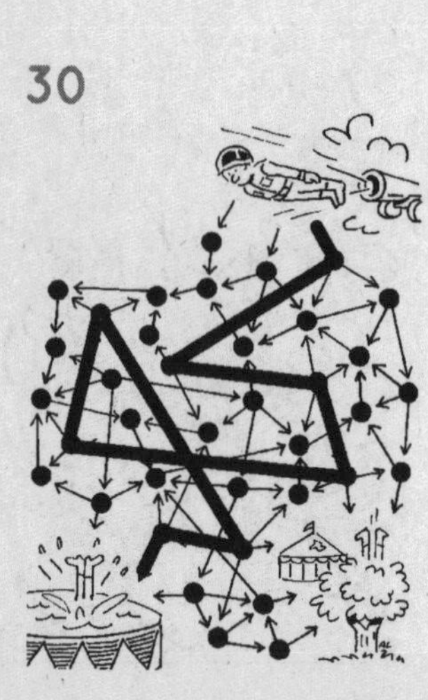

31

START

FINISH

32

LOST!

WRONG WAY!

33

34

START

FINISH

35

36

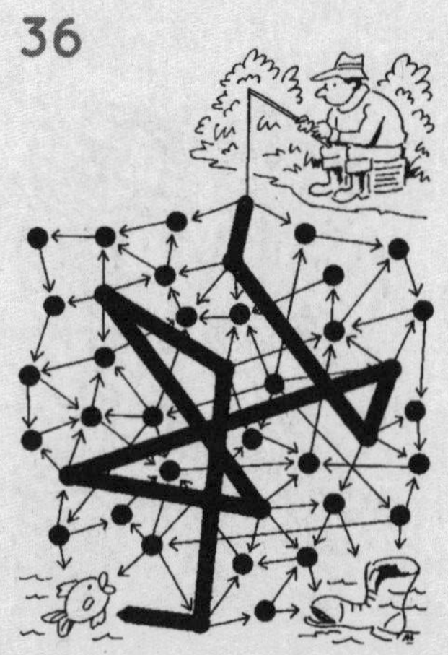

37

40

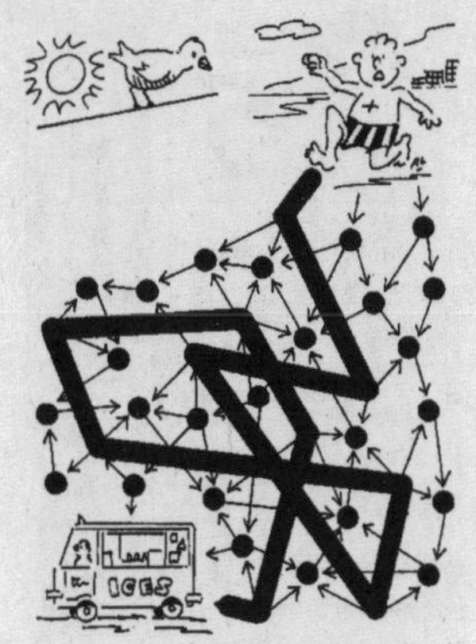

43

38

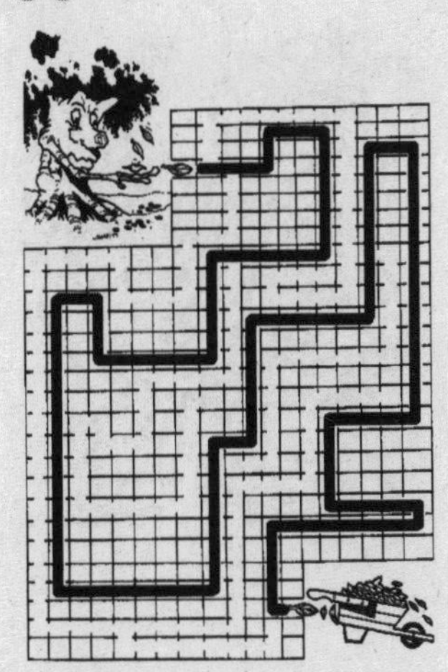

41

44

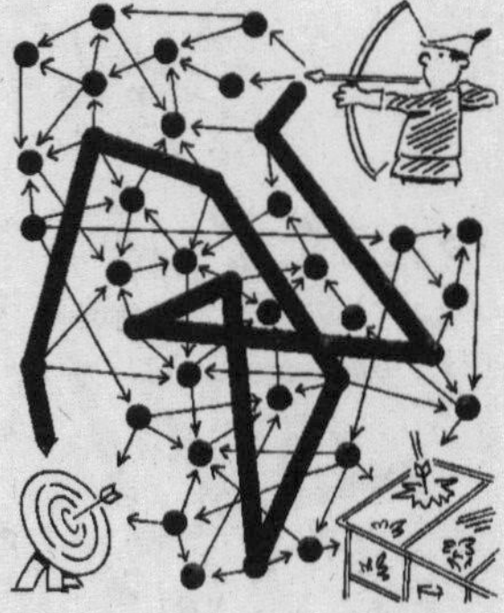

39

42

45

46

START.

FINISH.

49

52

47

50

53

48

51

54

55

56

57

START.

58

FINISH.

59

60

61

62

START

FINISH

63

64

65

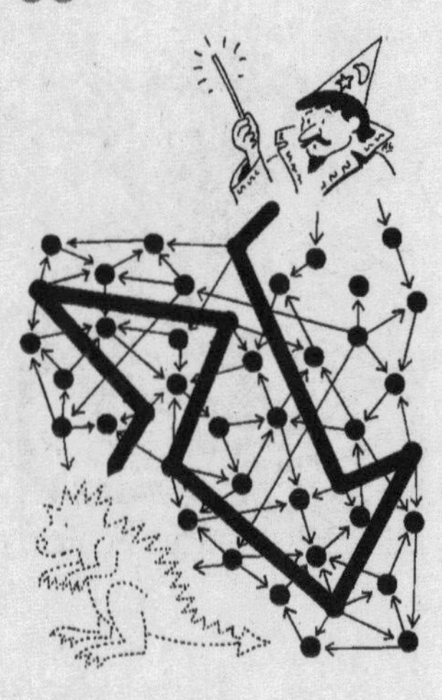

66

67

68

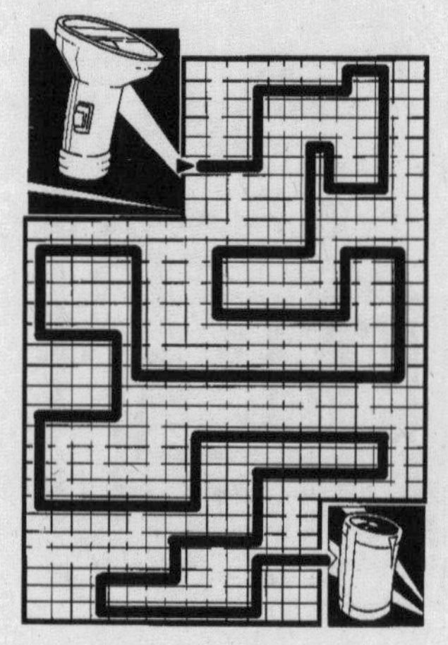

69

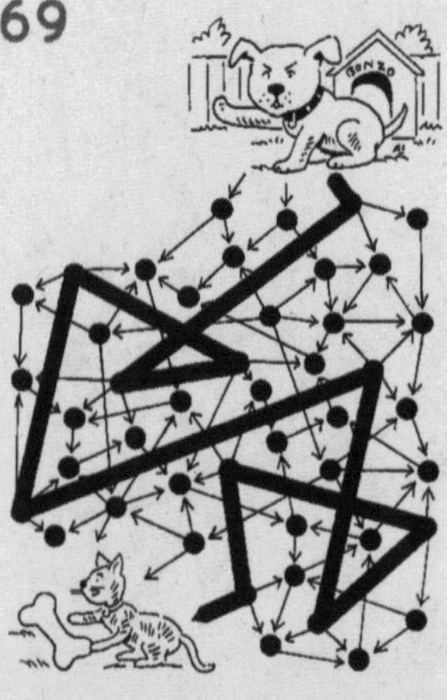

70

71

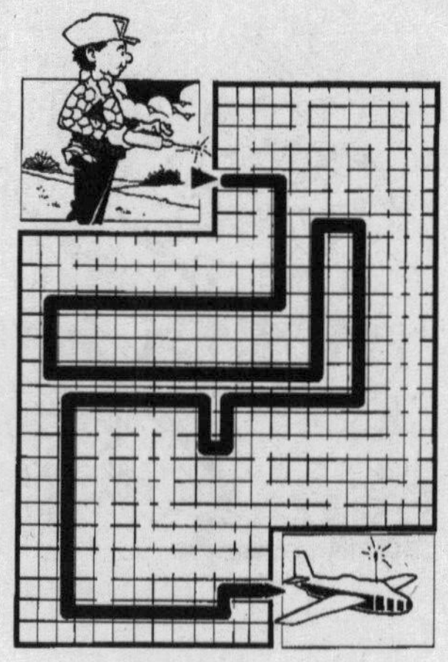

72

73

74

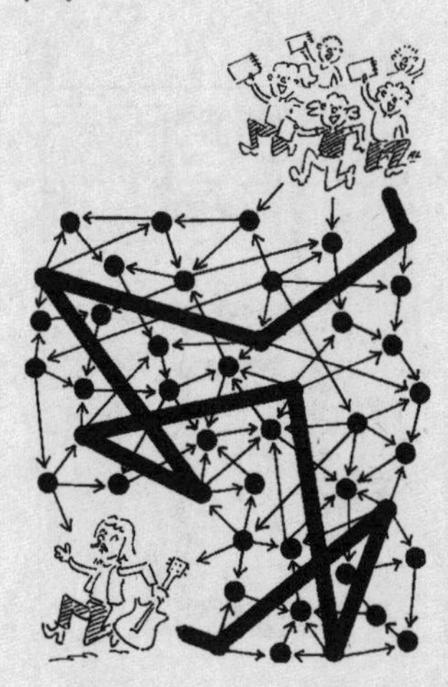

75

76

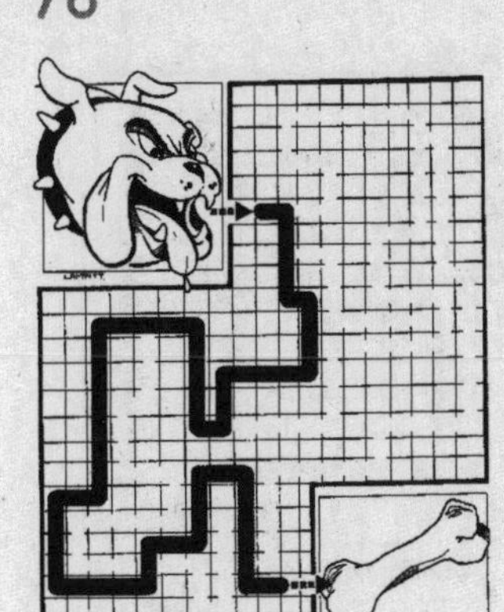

77

78

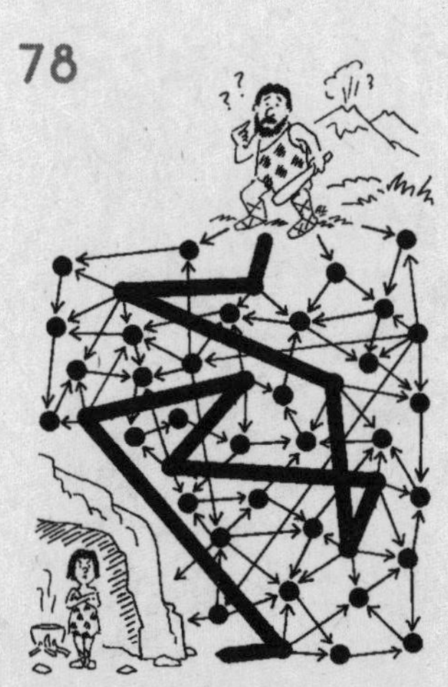

79

80

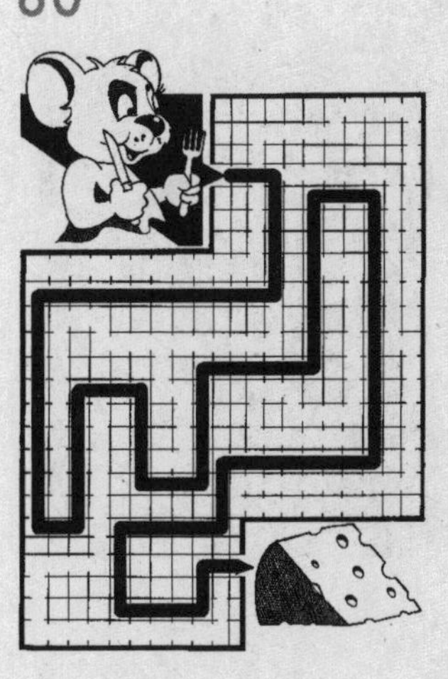

81

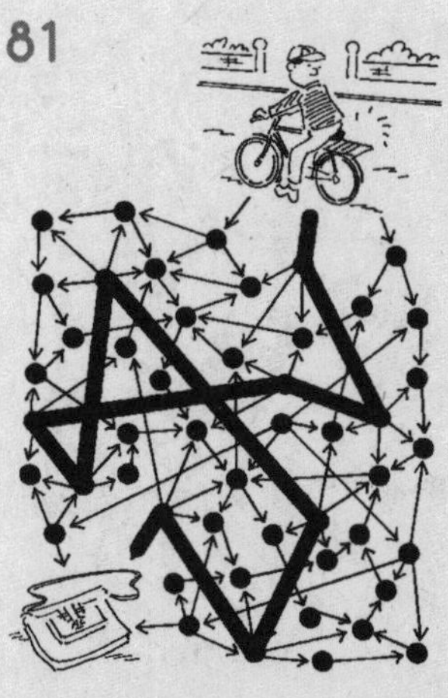

82

83

84

85

86

START.

FINISH.

87

88

START.

FINISH.

89

90

91

92

93

94

95

96

97

98

99

100

103

106

101

104

UG'S CAVE

107

START.

FINISH.

102

105

108

FINISH

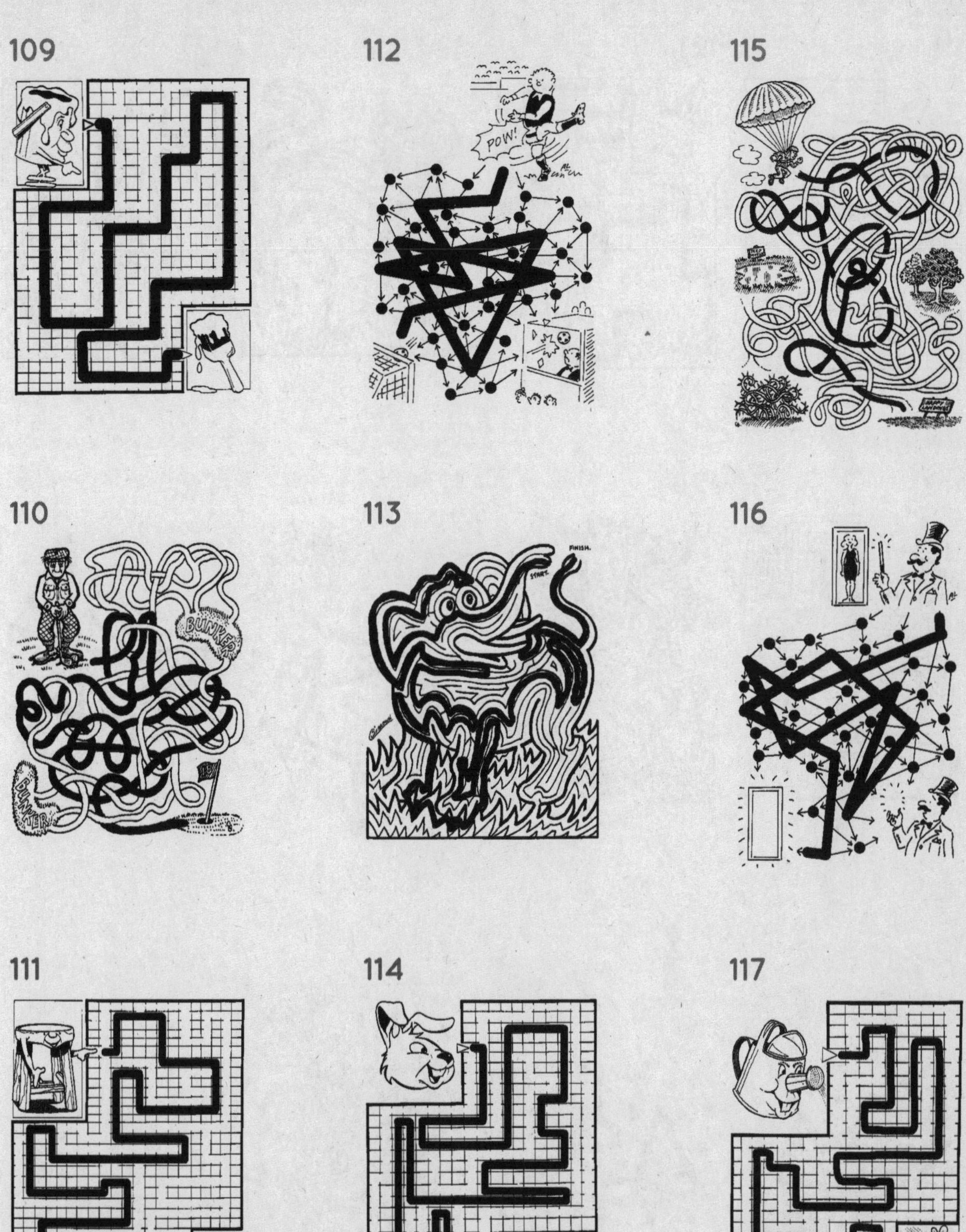

109
112
115
POW!
110
113
116
BUNKER
BUNKER
FINISH.
START.
111
114
117

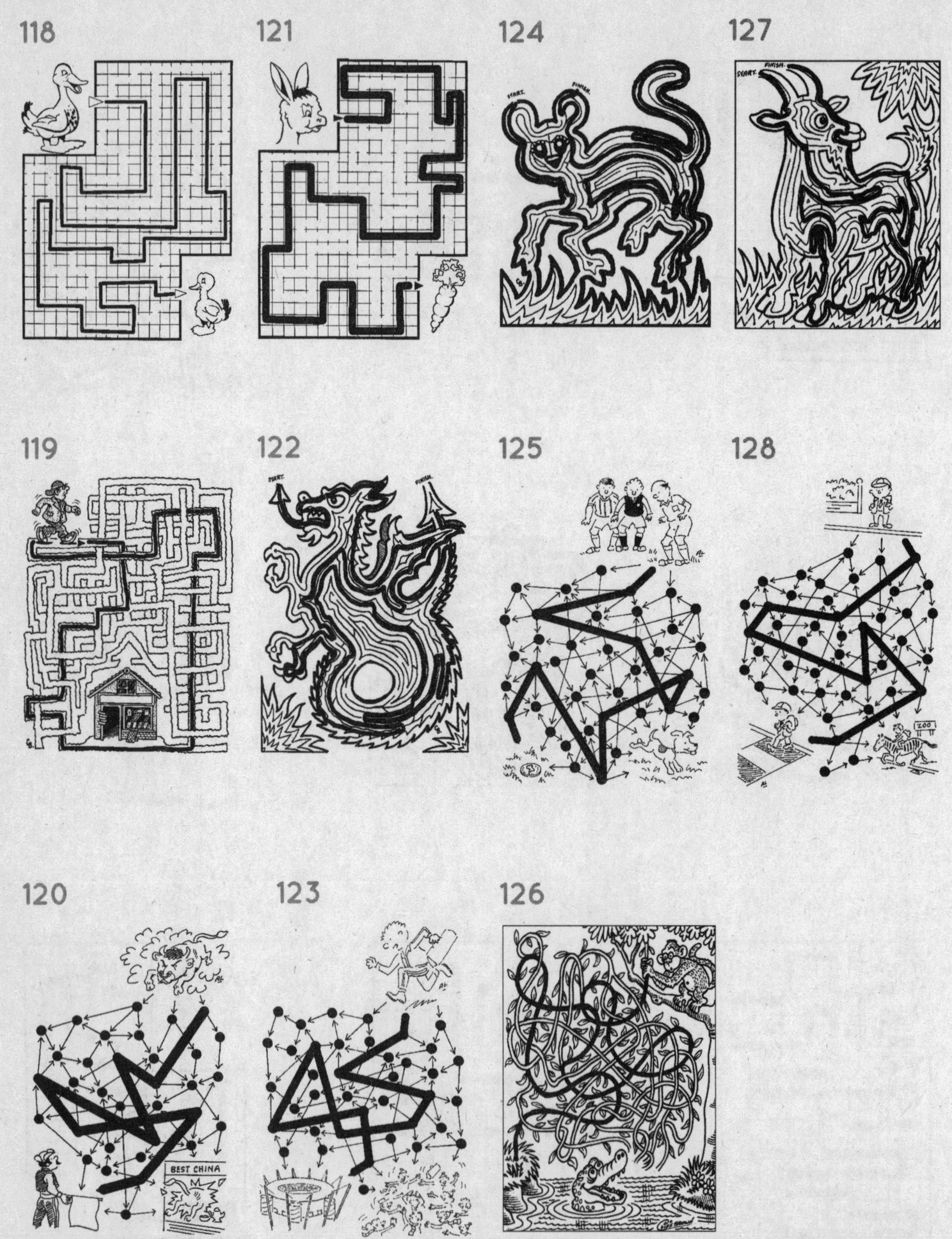

118
121
124
START.
FINISH.
127
START.
FINISH.
119
122
START.
FINISH.
125
128
ZOO
120
BEST CHINA
123
126